WELCOME TO THE U.S.A.

YOU'RE HIRED!

A GUIDE FOR FOREIGN-BORN
PEOPLE SEEKING JOBS

BETSY H. COHEN

CP
CONSTEAD
PRESS

Welcome to the U.S.A. – You're Hired!

Copyright © 2021 by Betsy H. Cohen

All rights reserved, including the right to reproduce this book or portions thereof in any form whatsoever. For information about using parts of this book or for bulk purchases, contact: Betsy Cohen at betsy@welcomeyouarehired.com

Project Managed by: Bonnie Daneker at The Author's Greenhouse

Copyediting by: Andrew Doty at Editwright

Cover and Interior Design by: Becky Bayne at Becky's Graphic Design

Manufactured in the United States of America

Library of Congress Cataloging-in-Publication Data

Name: Elizabeth H. Cohen

Title: Welcome to the U.S.A. – You're Hired!

Description: A Guide For Foreign-Born People Seeking Jobs

Library of Congress Control Number: 2021913996

ISBN: 978-1-7375453-0-9 (Trade Paperback)

ISBN: 978-1-7375453-1-6 (eBook)

Classification:

Business: Job Search, Career Advice

To the success of foreign-born job seekers as they make the U.S.A. a better place for all of us.

"The struggle to find a job – the *right* job – is very real in the U.S. especially for foreign-born job applicants. For success, applicants must frequently set-aside their previous job-hunting knowledge and experience to learn anew. Counselors and supporters can be challenged by navigating the labyrinth of market resources and advice not necessarily developed with the linguistic and cultural challenges of the foreign-born worker in mind. During my 42-year career working with immigrant newcomers, I was keenly aware of the lack of reliable authoritative materials that tackled such issues and needs.
Now, along comes *Welcome to the U.S.A – You're Hired!* The author, Betsy Cohen, Founding Executive Director of the St. Louis Mosaic Project, along with a number of contributing experts, has expertly laid out the search, hiring and post-hiring process to ease the process and improve opportunities. Don't wait. Buy this book today."

ANNA CROSSLIN

President & CEO emeritus, International Institute of St. Louis

....

"Moving to a new country and re-starting your career can feel like an enormous mountain to climb. This book gives you a map, a compass, and a backpack full of supplies. Previous generations of newcomers have struggled to put together this kind of information bit by bit. Today, books like this one provide a vital overview, making it possible for you to instead focus your energy on choosing the most rewarding opportunities. May you and your talents flourish in the United States!"

AMANDA BERGSON-SHILCOCK

Immigration advocate

....

"International students who want to work in the United States should consider this book. It includes advice on important issues that will help you understand the key issues you need to know to search for a job in the United States and share your talent. Our students have benefited from the knowledge in this book over the past years as we have worked with the team at the St. Louis Mosaic Project."

KURT DIRKS
Washington University in St. Louis, Vice Chancellor for International Affairs and Director of the McDonnell International Scholars Academy

....

"As the fastest growing, most profitable cohort in the country, Hispanics need to be able to access the best information to succeed when searching for a job or seeking advancement. The advice in this book helps demystify the application and interview processes. One of the pillars of the Hispanic Promise, the first-of-its-kind corporate pledge supporting the community, is preparation. It is crucial to have strategies and partnerships to support the future pipeline of Hispanic talent and this book represents an important resource to achieve this."

CLAUDIA ROMO EDELMAN
Founder of We Are All Human

....

"For businesses to thrive and grow in America today they need a rapidly expanding, hardworking, enterprising workforce. Attracting and retaining foreign-born talent will be critical to the success of their strategy and competitiveness in the 21st Century. *Welcome to the U.S.A. — You're Hired!* provides new immigrants access to nationally-known experts to help them along the way, greatly accelerating their entry into the workforce of today and tomorrow."

BOB FOX
Co-Founder of the St. Louis Mosaic Project

....

TESTIMONIALS

"As communities across the U.S. grapple with demographic shifts and economic challenges, this book offers a collection of current best practices in promoting economic growth through immigrant integration. This enables the foreign-born job seeker to improve job success. If you are a policy-maker, an employer, or a community developer working to understand and change barriers—this book is a must read."

PETER GONZALES
President and CEO of The Welcoming Center

....

"Relocation to the U.S. is an important career opportunity for many families. This book is a needed guide for the accompanying partners who will be seeking jobs during their time here. The book addresses the stress of the job search, a topic I have also written about and believe is critical to master."

LAUREN HERRING
CEO of IMPACT Group and author of Take Control of Your Job Search!

....

"I have been committed to helping foreign-born people come to our community and be successful in their lives. This book offers the advice of many experts and will help these important contributors navigate the U.S. job market. The growing American economy needs talent that our foreign-born community brings to our workplace. This book is a unique contribution of advice for an increasingly important part of our population."

DAVID KEMPER
Chairman of Commerce Bank

....

"This book will serve as a great guide to both foreign-born as well as to native-born job seekers as they navigate through the job seeking process here in the United States. To understand employer expectations, in addition to what works and what doesn't work, I highly recommend that every job seeker read this book."

BOB KOLF
Founder & CEO, Job Seekers' Garden Club of St. Louis

....

"Across the United States, the Asian immigrant population is very diverse in terms of ethnicity, language, and culture, but these communities share a common aspiration to succeed in the U.S.A. This book provides important case studies and tips that offer our varied communities great guidance on how to successfully navigate the job search process and positively advance in one's career."

ALEX LEE
Co-Founder/President of the Asian-American Chamber of Commerce of St. Louis

....

"Betsy Cohen and other experts have written the definitive guide to entering the American workforce for foreign-born professionals at all stages of their careers. Especially for readers interested in joining the startup or innovation economies across America, this book will serve as a guide for both you and your employers to more confidently manage the legal, social, and professional hurdles that make it difficult for immigrants to fully contribute to their new hometowns and the American economy generally. Economic development leaders might find this book helpful to better understand the problems faced by and craft solutions for support of foreign-born communities seeking to contribute to your region's growth in building a more vibrant future."

CRAIG MONTUORI
Executive Director at Global EIR

....

"The United States wants you. Communities like St. Louis need you. With labor in short supply and slow domestic population growth, attracting and retaining talent from around the globe is more important than ever in an increasingly interconnected global economy. For the first time ever, Betsy Cohen and a collection of experts provide the valuable tips and insights to help launch your new career in the United States. You will bring your knowledge of the wider world to your U.S. community, making it better for all of us."

TIM NOWAK
Executive Director of the World Trade Center St. Louis

....

"The Hispanic community is growing and filling more jobs at all levels. Through cultural and business organizations we are building a support network. The case studies and advice from experts in this book show the insider knowledge our community needs to advance in the interview and career advancement process."

KARLOS RAMÍREZ,
President and CEO of the Hispanic Chamber of Commerce of Metropolitan St. Louis

....

"Originally from Mexico and inspired by my own experiences growing up an immigrant in the United States, I am passionate and committed to helping people in marginalized communities have access to opportunities for wealth creation. I am excited for the insight and support shared in this book so that others like me, can find success in their job searches without the frustration of not understanding the different operating procedures of the US job market. What a great way to encourage, inspire and prepare job seekers!"

GABRIELA RAMÍREZ-ARELLANO
Director of Entrepreneurship at Cortex Innovation Community and Hispanic/Diversity Business Catalyst

....

"While so much of immigration policy and immigration advocacy has focused almost exclusively on who gets to come here, Betsy Cohen has been a pioneer in shedding light on and opening doors for immigrants after they arrive. Her deep experience assisting immigrants in breaking into the workforce and building strong social networks make her and the other experts she has enlisted for the book a gold mine for practical wisdom on what immigrants really need to succeed and thrive in America."

JEREMY ROBBINS
Executive Director, New American Economy

....

"The United States was the top destination for talent—essentially by default—from around the world for over a century, but that is no longer the case. America needs an aggressive strategy to welcome immigrants and to ensure they can be successful in joining the workforce—and this guide is a tremendous asset in this effort."

TODD SCHULTE
President - FWD.us

....

"There are many books on finding a good immigration lawyer, but few on how to find a good job if you have a work visa or green card. This book fills that gap. It provides useful information on how finding a job in the United States may differ from other countries. Everyone should buy it."

STEPHEN YALE-LOEHR
Professor of Immigration Practice, Cornell Law School and Of Counsel, Miller Mayer LLP

....

Table of Contents

Testimonials v

Foreword xv

Introduction.. xix

STAGE I: UNDERSTANDING THE JOB SEARCH 1

Foreign-Born vs. Native-Born Job Seeker...................................... 1

   Understanding the Job-Search Process in a New Environment ... 3

   Presenting Your Skills... 4

   Interviewing 5

   The Stress of Waiting 5

   Advancing in Your Job 9

   Preserving Family Relationships 9

   Uncertainty of Timing for a Future Move 10

Managing the Stress 13

   Keep a Positive Attitude.. 14

   Structure Your Search Time 15

   Gather the Support of Friends 15

   Have a Coach or Mentor.. 16

STAGE II: PRE-JOB INTERVIEW TOOLS AND TIPS............... 19

Your American Résumé vs. the CV (Curriculum Vitae) 19

   How to Structure Your Résumé... 23

   Which Name Should You Use? 26

The Cover Letter and Your Submitted Application 33

The Importance of Your U.S. Network 36

The Role of Networking vs. Posted Job Opportunities 44

The "Warm Introduction" 47

Using LinkedIn and Other Professional Networks 51

Business Cards and Other Professional Materials 55

STAGE III: INTERVIEW PROCESSES AND PREPARATION 61

Interview Types: *Pre-Interviewing Screening,*
One Person Interview, Panel Interviews 63

Interview Types: Chronological and Behavioral 67

Interview Components That Are Most Important in the U.S. 73

    Skills 75

    Attitude 75

References 81

Resilience and Response 83

Visa and Work Authorization Discussions 85

Additional Work Experience: *Projects, Internships,*
Mentorships, and Job Shadowing 89

Thank-You Letters to Employers and Those
Who Gave Assistance 93

STAGE IV: ACCEPTING A JOB OFFER 99

Job Offers and Negotiations 101

Using Immigration Lawyers 103

STAGE V: ADVANCING YOUR WORKPLACE CAREER 112

Quality Interactions with Colleagues 112

Sponsors and Mentors 117

Support Networks in a Company 120

Highlight Your Performance and Contributions
to Get Promotions and Pay Increases 124

Diversity, Equity, and Inclusion (DEI) at Work 128

STAGE VI: SPECIAL KNOWLEDGE 137

    International Students 137

    Refugees 147

    Transferred Spouses/Partners... 154

    Professional Connections at the Executive Level..............................164

    LinkedIn Expertise in Depth 171

    Credentials 176

    Upwardly Global 182

    Conclusion 187

ACKNOWLEDGMENTS 189

ABOUT THE AUTHOR 193

RESOURCES..195

EXPERT CONTRIBUTORS

    Résumés: Anita Barker, International Institute of St. Louis — immigrant services and community engagement hub since 1919 (www.iistl.org)

    Connections: Susanne Evens, AAA Translation

    Immigration Attorney: Nalini Mahadevan, MLO Law, LLC, immigration attorney

    Diversity, Equity, and Inclusion at Work: Sharon Harvey Davis, Ameren, Living Our Values in Uncertain Times — www.Ameren.com

    International Students: Guiqiu Wang and Steve Tobocman, Global Detroit, Global Talent Retention Initiative — (https://globaldetroitmi.org)

    Refugees: Chelsea Hand-Sheridan, International Institute of St. Louis — immigrant services and community engagement hub since 1919 (www.iistl.org)

    Transferred Spouses/Partners: Susan Gobbo, St. Louis International Spouses Meetup Group; Annie Schlafly, International Mentoring

Program — St. Louis, St. Louis Mosaic Project Women's Connector (www.stlmosaicproject.org)

(www.stlmosaicproject.org/womens-connector.html)

(www.itspouses.org)

Professional Connections: Ram Lakshmanan, Executive Connections St. Louis, Executive Connections St. Louis (www.executiveconnectionsstl.org)

LinkedIn: Kathy Bernard, WiserU — LinkedIn and Career Trainer and www.linkedin.com/in/kathybernard

Credentials: Paul Feltman, Global Talent Bridge, World Education Services (www.wes.org)

Upwardly Global: The Upwardly Global Team, immigrant and refugee professionals career services (www.upwardlyglobal.org)

Foreword

I first met Betsy Cohen when I was introduced to her and her work through the St. Louis Mosaic Project, an initiative focused on weaving immigrant Americans into the rich tapestry of St. Louis and growing the region's population to address many years of exodus. The work was ambitious, visionary, and audacious — just like Betsy Cohen.

As I got to know Betsy through her work in St. Louis, and later as a board member for my organization, Welcoming America, I came to know her as a determined leader with a generous spirit, always eager to use her network expansively to connect people to opportunity, and to use her position and power to expand the potential of others to do great things. While many people willingly extend this kind of support to those similar to them, Betsy deliberately focuses on people born outside the U.S., whose networks — and therefore opportunities — are often more limited.

At a time when too many leaders profit from seeing the world in zero-sum terms, Betsy's instinct to champion those with boundless talent but limited opportunity offers a powerful alternative — an abundant vision in which we rise together.

Finding a job in America — and navigating the unwritten norms and culture of the marketplace of work — is a daunting task for any jobseeker, and certainly for those who are the first generation to arrive here. More daunting yet are the unnecessary barriers that stand in the way of success, from bias and systemic racism to an outmoded approach to credentialing, to the challenges of transportation, childcare, and other issues faced by millions of American workers, new and longtime alike. The particular challenges of language, customs, of translating expertise and experience, and building networks that extend beyond our own peer group, are ones that many immigrant Americans must navigate, often with little support or even empathy.

As the executive director of an organization that works with communities to bring down these barriers and create an environment in which each of us — including immigrants — can thrive, belong, and prosper, I know just what this book can offer. It can unlock the hidden talent and contributions of Americans born outside the U.S. It can also point to remedying the barriers and biases that hinder the potential of every American. While diversity may be a fact of the American workforce, its ability to be fully unleashed in the service of our creativity, innovation, and ability to solve problems together is far from our current reality. But we have the power to change that, and I imagine many readers of this book could be among those who do.

If you're an immigrant American reading this book, I want you to know that there are many of us rooting for you to succeed, despite the politics and narratives that suggest otherwise. Your success is our shared success as a nation that can see the potential of every person determined by what we do, not where we come from, what we look like, how we pray, or who we love. There are millions of Americans who not only believe in these ideals but want to see them lived out in the workplace, in neighborhoods, and in our democracy. This work — the work of building a welcoming community — often begins with the simple actions that each of us can take to lift up ourselves and others toward shared success.

Nowhere is that more important and urgent than when it comes to the dignity of a job for every American, whether we've been here for generations or have arrived more recently. Readers of this book will find practical advice, tools, ideas, and support to succeed as individuals. They'll find evidence of the abundance of champions who, like Betsy, are eager to see us build a culture in which our shared humanity and unique talents are put to good use, creating communities where all of us rise together.

RACHEL PERIĆ
Executive Director, Welcoming America
www.welcomingamerica.org

Introduction

When I was growing up, our family lived in St. Louis, Missouri. My single mom wanted to expose my two brothers and me to the global world, so we became members of an international welcoming organization in town. As part of that, we had international guests come to our home for dinner occasionally. This inspired me to live with a French family over the summer of my junior year of high school. I took my guitar and sang my way through France, making friends and improving my language skills. I used the name "Elise" while living in France, as "Betsy" was not a common name there. I tried to dress and act like a true French teenager. Later, in college and when getting my MBA, I gravitated to the international student organizations and dreamed of working for an international company.

I had a wonderful career in marketing, new business development, e-commerce, and new products for a largely U.S.-based company. I was so excited when the largest food company in the world acquired my employer in 2002 and I was able to visit the global headquarters in Switzerland. Of course, I used my French language skills on the train as we rode past Lake Geneva.

Several highlights of my corporate career were international business trips. I worked on global environmental sustainability issues with international colleagues. I mentored international associates who moved to St. Louis. My company even asked me to form and lead a St. Louis coalition that used my local networks and marketing skills.

In 2013, I left my corporate career and took a position as founding executive director for a public–private partnership housed within our regional economic development organization. The job of the executive director of the St. Louis Mosaic Project is to attract and retain foreign-born people to our region. I learned that those in the immigration community call these people "foreign-born" to represent all of those in the country who were born outside the United States, and that those born in the United States are called "native-born." I also learned that in the university and corporate communities these people are often referred to as "internationals." You may also see the word "immigrant" used to refer to someone who comes to the U.S. And a refugee is a special kind of immigrant. I will use these terms throughout my discussions.

In these past years, I have worked with hundreds of foreign-born job seekers. I have helped them to connect to their professional networks, to broaden their skills, and to modify their approach to the U.S. job market. This work of job connections has been done with many regional partners. Because of these learnings, many of the international people I know kept telling me to write this book. They wanted me to share with more people what I have told them, and they wanted the knowledge I have been sharing on LinkedIn® to be collected in one place to be used more easily. In this book, I have done just that.

The focus of this book is on those job seekers who are already authorized to work here long-term and do not need visa sponsorship from their employers. You will see examples, or "case studies," so that you may learn from their experiences. All names have been changed, but the stories you will read about are true and shared from my personal experiences. Near the end of this book, you will see specialized chapters to address those who have different paths to employment in the United States, including international students, spouses/partners of those transferred to the U.S. for work, refugees, and others. There is also advanced material for those seeking higher-level jobs. This collection of experiences originated in different settings, and where I have used "we," "us" and "our," I am referring to those who worked with me in my various work-related or volunteer-related organizations.

With a growing percentage of the United States being foreign-born, plus new, incoming internationals seeking jobs and career advancement, many job seekers can benefit from the knowledge in this book. Our country has close to 1 million international students. This book may also help job seekers who are already U.S. citizens, such as workers from Puerto Rico looking for suggestions for their job searches and career success.

There are many reasons that immigrant talent is needed in our country. The United States' economic growth will depend both on less-skilled jobs that native-born workers choose not to do as well as high-skilled STEM openings that the U.S. cannot train native-born workers fast enough to fill. There will also be jobs requiring global business/language skills. In addition, we now know that many jobs can be done remotely, so there will be a real need to attract and retain talent in the U.S. as some talent trained here goes to work overseas.

The United States increasingly has companies and organizations seeking to build more diverse, inclusive workplaces. This means developing our African American communities and the talents there. It also means seeking to attract, hire, and develop the talents of other people of color — many of whom are immigrants or children of immigrants — and Caucasian immigrants as well. You, our foreign-born job seekers, will be an important part of building a diverse and inclusive workforce in our country. You will add to the workplace that our progressive companies are seeking to develop. In short, now is a particularly good time for your job search.

My passion is to help as many foreign-born people as possible in the United States to find jobs and careers that benefit them and the United States economy. That is why I felt it was so important to share what I have learned. You may have additional experiences to share as well. If you think your ideas or experience would help others, let me know, and I will consider incorporating your advice in future editions or updates. Please write me at **betsy@welcomeyouarehired.com**.

Best of luck to you,
BETSY COHEN

STAGE I:

Understanding the Job Search

Welcome to your job search process! This is an exciting time in your life. You want to get a new job — or a better job — in America. You have overcome many challenges to get to this point in your life. You have developed your English skills for the U.S. marketplace. You have read about how your specific work field operates in the United States and reviewed the related English vocabulary for your field. You have work authorization or expect to have that in the coming months. Now you're ready!

FOREIGN-BORN VS. NATIVE-BORN JOB SEEKER

In this book, you will find tips to make your job search process as smooth as possible. This means you will read about both the emotional and the factual aspects of the job search process. Being a foreign-born candidate means that you bring additional global skills and language to your work. It also means that you are competing with native-born job seekers who have an advantage of knowing the American system. Inside these pages is the best advice from many international job seekers who have successfully moved into the U.S. workforce. By learning from them, you can understand the steps of the process and shorten the time of your job search. You will feel more in control of your life and your work.

Let's look at an example where a native-born colleague was helping his foreign-born colleague due to the unusual stress of the visa situation.

Case Study

HIMADRI, A PROCESS ENGINEER FROM INDIA

Himadri had an employer-sponsored visa but was facing a workforce layoff. He needed to find another employer. He was referred to us by one of his work colleagues, and there was stress in the colleague's voice as he sought to help this talented international person find workplace options. There was also a sense of worry, of stress, in Himadri's voice. The advising team tried to convey optimism to both that through networking and making more good connections, a solution would be found. He received an introduction to a company that would appreciate his technical skills. Two days later, the candidate wrote that a strong connection had been made and he was optimistic about a new work option. The following week, he received a job offer and confirmation that his visa could be transferred. There was relief in his tone when he shared his good news.

In these human situations, remember that the stress around a job search is real, and it can be quite high. There are different stressors for every international job seeker: the job search process in a new environment, the need to show professional skills in a new country, the act of interviewing, advancing in a different work culture, and the stress on family/personal relationships. Let's look at each of these.

UNDERSTANDING THE JOB-SEARCH PROCESS IN A NEW ENVIRONMENT

It is no surprise the upcoming job search is stressful to even think about, much less begin. At the same time, you are probably getting yourself (and possibly family members) settled into a new living arrangement. They have needs as well. If you are the accompanying partner of someone making a work move to the United States, it likely falls on you to get all family members into a solid home situation, find schools, and help get work for other family members. You must establish new shopping, medical/dental, and grocery options. You may want to find a new religious congregation. You will want to make your first friends or add to your circle of friends. Whether or not you can speak English fluently, acclimating can take months.

In addition to learning about your new home life, you need to learn about a new job search environment. This is an extra level of stress that you bear which a native-born job seeker does not. The job search process is always stressful, especially when you do not know the streets, buildings, or companies. Try to appreciate and manage your extra stress level so that you can effectively complete a job search that can take some time to achieve.

PRESENTING YOUR SKILLS

In your home country, you knew the right way to do a CV and a résumé. Maybe it was common to get a job introduction and job offer directly through your network of family friends or university connections. It's likely that everyone knew the name and reputation of your university. They understood the training you accomplished.

In America, you must show your professional skills in a different way. You will discover differences in technology or processes that may be easier or frustrating. For example, when you fill out an online job application there is no drop-down menu option for your university, you have no zip codes to put into the spaces for your prior employment, and the titles of your prior job description do not seem the same as a similar job in the U.S.

There was one job seeker who had worked on pensions and benefits for the government in a socialist country, and the description of her work on her original résumé did not align with jobs here. Eventually, her work was able to be described in terms that fit with what the U.S. workforce calls "human resources and benefits" skills. The St. Louis Mosaic Project arranged for her to do a work-shadowing experience for a few days, an opportunity set up with a local human resources (HR) professional. She spent time observing the human resources worker doing her job, like a shadow. That started to relieve her stress of determining what her professional career might look like.

You may have to shadow, as mentioned above, or even volunteer in an organization to see if it is right for you. Another job seeker with a master's degree from Syria took a volunteer position in a lab to get relevant updated skills, which led to a full-time job offer once they saw her work ability. She has still not reached her prior professional level but does have a good job with benefits. The same can happen to you as you build your support network and find resources.

INTERVIEWING

In your home country, you knew how to present yourself when called to interview for a job. You knew how to dress, what to say or not say, and how to follow up with the conversation. Suddenly, it is all different! Later sections in this book will lighten your stress.

It takes personal resilience and patience to wait for the actual interview process and an offer to occur. How else can you keep up your spirits and resilience during the job search process? Let's look at that waiting situation so you are prepared for it mentally.

THE STRESS OF WAITING

Your job interview and offer process can take much longer than you hoped. Or it can happen very quickly. This variation can cause you a lot of stress in different ways. Let's look at some examples.

Case Studies

FERNANDA, A SENIOR FINANCE LEADER FROM BRAZIL

Fernanda had applied to a large company. She went through three rounds of interviews over a month. She was ready to get the offer. But she heard nothing. When she emailed to inquire about an update, an HR professional told Fernanda that the process was on hold but still positive. This made Fernanda nervous. Should she wait for the offer or start talking to other companies? Was the company as good as she had previously thought? Were they not interested and just keeping her waiting? She was stressed out and increased her daily running routine to deal with this. Her husband was tired of hearing about it. Her work at her current company was stagnating. She kept waiting and finally got the offer a month later.

HANNAH, AN IT MANAGER FROM GERMANY

Hannah heard about a job at a small startup that was growing rapidly. Through the introduction of a friend to the company owner, she had an interview on a Monday. She was enthused by what she learned of the company's growth and plans. On Friday, four days later, she received an offer. She was surprised by how quickly it had all happened. She was not sure if she should accept, as she had not been looking around at any other companies to see what else might be available. Her current job was going well, and she was in the middle of a big project with deliverables in several weeks. She was confused about what she should do.

You'll notice that in the first case study the job offer was very delayed and that caused one kind of stress. In the second case the job offer came so quickly that it resulted in a different kind of stress. While getting a quick offer seems like it would not create stress, it really might provoke a new kind of stress. Remember that you can have all kinds of stress in the job search process. Do not be surprised by this variation in what is possible.

Often, U.S. job searches take a long time. In fact, the search can take six to twelve months. You will usually find that during the interview process there is a lot of waiting time for American companies. For a large company with over 500 employees, it can take two weeks for each step of a multiple-interview process. There may be outside testing as well for skills, attitude, or aptitude. Even after all that, it can take four to eight weeks for a company to get all the internal approvals to make you an offer. The wait can seem endless. You need to be prepared for that.

In a smaller company, the process can move quickly. So think about the implications for your work and personal life if an offer is very delayed and the opposite situation if you get an offer very quickly. While a fast offer is likely to be a good sign of your employability and job success, it does create a different stress of its own.

Why This Works

You need mental toughness to deal with the job search. There are often many steps and assessments. There can be different people and layers of management involved in your decision, such as the hiring manager who would be your boss, the hiring manager's boss, the HR team, or the financial team that approves staffing budgets. And there may be other complications, such as a downturn in the overall business that necessitates a hold on new hires or a hiring freeze to delay any new hires or promotions until the new year's budget starts.

Remember that you may be waiting because there are other candidates or because the company is going through something beyond your control or the control of the hiring manager. You can check in with the person who is your main contact each week or two with a nice email inquiring "Is there any update on the process?" or "What might be our next steps?" Regardless of what you hear, stay pleasant and calm. Keep as many other aspects of your life as calm as possible so you are not stressed by things like moving homes or new roommates at the same time. Patience will win the game if you understand it can take months to get to your job offer in the U.S.

ADVANCING IN YOUR JOB

After you start a job, the relationships in the workplace could give you different stress and anxiety. Questions arise, such as: What do people do for lunch as colleagues? Why is golf important? Why does doing a good job not get you promoted to a new role when you see others get promoted who do not work as hard? A new workplace and different career development expectations present stress levels that are not to be ignored but can be managed.

PRESERVING FAMILY RELATIONSHIPS

Family relationships can be strained when you move and seek a job in the U.S. As a job seeker, your anxiety may be best managed with the support of others who can assist you in the job search process by being compassionate and offering pathways to solutions. Maybe your spouse does not understand as you struggle to learn how to manage computer job applications, online testing, video interviews, and networking sites like LinkedIn. He does not understand why you keep applying and do not get responses. Or she doesn't want to hear any more about the recruiter who told you the company was extremely interested and then did not call you back. Your time will be spent attending networking events, which may make quick dinners necessary for your family.

Pay attention to the stress levels of family members and your own stress level. For yourself, find ways to relieve that stress, such as a daily walk, a tea break, or a planned call with family across the world. You'll see more suggestions on ways to reduce stressful situations later in this book.

UNCERTAINTY OF TIMING FOR A FUTURE MOVE

Most native-born job seekers have a good idea of the timing of their graduation from a university or when they will move to a new city. For international families, this may not be the case. The international family may need to move suddenly due to a change in the employer's need for the worker to be in another country, or a visa change may require a need to change countries. A foreign-born spouse may be waiting for a work authorization certificate from the U.S. government that does not arrive when expected. You need to understand that expectations for a job search may need to shift.

Let's look at what happened to a woman who had customer service experience but uncertainty in her life planning.

Case Study:

GUADALUPE, A CUSTOMER SERVICE PROFESSIONAL FROM MEXICO

One of the companies the St. Louis Mosaic Project works with called to find a customer service professional. The team there referred Guadalupe, a woman who had moved here with her husband a year earlier. Guadalupe called and explained that she was worried about going ahead with an interview because there was a possibility that the family would need to return to Mexico in the coming year and she did not want to mislead the hiring company. She wanted to discuss if she should interview at all, should she interview but not disclose this, or should she interview and disclose the possibility? She was stressed and sleepless over the issue because she really wanted a job and to begin working.

She reviewed the situation. Moving was not a certainty, so it seemed like she should go ahead with the interview. The team talked with her about the benefits and disadvantages of disclosing the potential of the future move, that if she started working it might only be for a year or so. In her case, she decided to tell the hiring manager of the possibility and take the chance that she would be eliminated from being considered for the job. In fact, the hiring manager decided to hire her with the knowledge that it might only be for a year. A year later, the family is still in our town and a move is not yet on the horizon.

This is a good situation to talk over with a trusted advisor for your local market. There will always be uncertainties about how long any new hire will stay in the job. Will a better job come along? Will you need to revise your work schedule due to a family need? Will the company provide the growth you hoped? Many unpredictable issues can arise after you start working; sometimes it is best to just do the interview and accept the job if you feel there is a 60% or more chance you will stay. If you believe it is only a 50% or lower chance that you will be staying in town, then you should consider the factors and decide whether to start the interview process.

Why This Works

Hiring is increasing and unemployment will be low in the coming years. An employer will need to find someone to do a great job, and you may be the best candidate. If you are a great employee for a year, that may still be a good situation for the company and for you. And often, a move for your family does not happen as quickly as you think it will. With more jobs being done remotely, there might even be a possibility to keep working remotely for the employer if you must move after you have started. For these reasons, you should weigh carefully how much uncertainty you want to put into the job interview process by sharing your move possibilities with those who interview you.

Experience shows that people end up staying in the U.S. longer than they expected for many reasons, so moving ahead on a new job often makes good sense. For example, life situations can change, including illness of a spouse, divorce, or school enrollment. You should look out for your professional needs and your family's needs. You should give yourself a chance to improve your professional skills in the workplace as much as possible to prepare for long employment in the United States. Stay optimistic!

But how do you manage this stress on a day-to-day basis? In the next section, let's talk about staying calm in the process of making these difficult decisions.

MANAGING THE STRESS

Everyone has stress. But moving internationally and seeking a job in a new country is a unique kind of stress. Let's discuss how to plan for the emotions you may experience during the months it takes you to move into a job. Below, you can examine a situation where one spouse had a delayed entry into the job market.

Case Study:

CARMINA, A FASHION DESIGNER WHO MOVED WITH HER HUSBAND FROM ITALY

Carmina had moved due to her husband's job and was now seeking her own job. She had made the family's move happen and gotten the new home in order. The children were settled into school and starting to make friends. Her husband was happy in his new role. But she was sad and getting discouraged as it took so long to start her own job search. As part of her job search routine, Carmina started doing an online video yoga program for stress relief every day once the kids left for school. Having this time for herself gave her a better physical and mental outlook that improved her job-search process as well.

Here are four ways to manage your career stress: Keep a positive attitude, structure your search time, gather the support of friends, and have a coach or mentor in the process. These will help you to be your best!

KEEP A POSITIVE ATTITUDE

Your behavior and attitude will influence your approach to your career. Work to stay positive. It may be difficult but try to frame your situation in a positive angle, such as "I will make three connections today that will give me more knowledge about my ideal career," or "I will look for a job that is on the path to my ultimate job goal. I understand that it may take some time to achieve my goals, and that is okay." People can sense your attitude and are more receptive when you are positive.

STRUCTURE YOUR SEARCH TIME

Set up your personal schedule so that you manage your time and behavior for the job search. It is helpful if you can have a certain time of the day or week that you set aside for your job search. That way you can focus during the time you have established and use the rest of the day for other things. You will need scheduled time to research companies, write letters and thank-you emails, and make networking relationship connections. If you can, set up a desk or other space to keep all your materials together. You will have information about organizations and people you are researching, and you will want to be able to find them when you need them.

GATHER THE SUPPORT OF FRIENDS

Having at least one supportive friend outside your family is a great benefit. It is best if that person is already familiar with the American work environment. It would be good to ask that friend if you could set up a time to talk about your job search every few weeks on a schedule, so you have someone outside your family to share the positive and negative feelings about the process with. This also takes the full pressure off your family members as you work through the emotional aspects of being in a job search or seeking to change jobs.

HAVE A COACH OR MENTOR

Lastly, it is extremely helpful to have a coach or mentor during the process. This is someone you have a relationship with, or someone recommended to you, who has knowledge of job searching. It is a person already in the field or skill area you want to enter. It helps if this person knows the American system and has connections in the region for this role. This is not a paid relationship, but it is still a professional relationship. You might ask in your neighborhood, at the school where your kids are enrolled, or in a welcoming program for newcomers.

How do you find and get someone to be your mentor? If you see someone you think could help you, ask them, in person or via email, with words like, "Dear Susanna, I notice that you know a lot about the industry. It would be extremely helpful if you would agree to have a short monthly call with me to guide me as I search for a position in this industry. I will bring one or two good questions to each session and seek your guidance. Would you be able to do this with me?" If they say no, find someone else to ask. Many people like to be a mentor or coach. They likely benefited in their own career from someone who helped them, and they may want to give back to help others. It also keeps the mentor smart and connected with the concerns of newcomers in the workplace, so don't be afraid to look for one during your job search. These relationships often last for a year or longer and are fulfilling for both the mentor and the mentee.

These examples have shown you how to prepare yourself mentally for the American job market. International job seekers in the U.S. are a highly-motivated and talented group. You have taken many risks to get to this place in your life. You may have left your home country by choice. You may have been forced to leave by outside circumstances. You have resilience. You have perseverance. You have a strong desire to work in the U.S. Now is the time for you to move forward to get your American job.

SUMMARY OF STAGE I
Understanding the Job Search

1. Remember that this hiring process may be different from what you have experienced in the past.
2. Manage your stress so you can be your best for yourself and those around you.

In the next section, we will discuss how you can prepare in the pre-job interview portion of your search. With these tips, you will feel confident in moving forward toward the American job market.

USE THIS SPACE TO TAKE NOTES *about planning your job search and managing your emotions.*

STAGE II:

Pre–Job Interview Tools and Tips

It is exciting and scary to begin your job search. You want to be prepared for the U.S. job market. You want to have the right materials with the right words to show that you understand the job market.

Let's break this part of your job search into seven topics: The American résumé vs. the CV, cover letters, the importance of your U.S. network, the role of networking vs. posted job opportunities, the "warm introduction," LinkedIn and other professional networks, and business cards and other professional materials.

YOUR AMERICAN RÉSUMÉ VS. THE CV (CURRICULUM VITAE)

This first case is about the need to shift from using a CV to a résumé.

Case Study

YASMINE, A SOCIAL WORKER FROM LEBANON

Yasmine's work authorization was due to occur in the next few months, so she would be able to work at that point with no visa sponsorship needed. She was finishing her advanced studies and was starting her job search. She sent her six-page CV to be reviewed. One of the first things she learned about job searching was how to turn this into a U.S.-style résumé of just two pages. She was told that after creating a U.S.-style résumé, she should create a LinkedIn profile that aligned to the résumé. From an emotional point of view, she was frustrated that a whole different document would be needed. She resisted the fact that it takes time and multiple review sessions to get a résumé right. She was also told that she needed to be more patient with the process. She sighed and rolled her eyes, but she did understand the point. She took several days to get a well-written two-page résumé ready for her search. She had a U.S. friend review it. She also had someone from her university career service office review the résumé. That résumé was her ticket to success, and she received several interviews after submitting this résumé for job consideration.

Many international people send a CV when they apply for a job at the start of their job search. The CV is usually a detailed document filled with the person's academic and work history. It often includes academic papers, publications, talks, and sources where the person is quoted. A CV may be five pages long or even longer. This is the right document for applying for an academic, scientific, or medical position in the United States. But the CV might still need to be reviewed and modified by an expert in your field in the U.S. or by those in the academic advising area of your local university career office.

A CV is not the right document for applying for a job outside of an academic or scientific institution. Your CV will need to be converted to a résumé format if you are looking for a job in technology, business, non-profit organizations, and most other industries. A résumé is a one- to two-page document that gives a brief description of your job objective, education, work or professional experiences, and volunteer experiences. You need an American résumé of one page if you have fewer than approximately five years of work experience, and a maximum of two pages if you have more than five years of work experience. Then, you need to structure your résumé in a way that is correct for the job market here. There is one example in the Resources section at the end of this book.

Here are a few tips about some differences from résumés created outside the U.S.:

- You need to determine what the right name is for you to use to get the right results you want. "My name?" you may ask in a worried tone. Yes, you need to decide what you would like the American job market to call you so that the people who interview you will find it easy to say your name when they call you on the phone or introduce you in person to a colleague — and that name also needs to be on your CV or résumé. We'll talk about that a little more on page 24.

- A U.S. résumé cannot have a picture on it due to legal requirements about discrimination.

You should look at résumé websites that are available online to see the preferred style that will be read by the computers and artificial intelligence (AI) of the employers in your field. These computer programs and applicant tracking systems (ATS) scan your résumé to see if the exact words that describe your work activities, called keywords, match those same keywords in the job description. A human resources professional or hiring manager in the company you are considering will make the same assessment of your keywords when they review your résumé with your cover letter.

Now that you understand how résumés are used, we will discuss in the next segment how you want to structure the résumé so that the reader best understands your ambition, your prior work, and your accomplishments. It is often true that you, as an international person, may have had jobs not in your field along the way to get where you are today. These unrelated jobs do not necessarily contribute to your new job goal, so structuring the résumé takes some different skills, which we will discuss next so you can show your best skills and advantages. You have so much to offer and need to show that in your materials!

HOW TO STRUCTURE YOUR RÉSUMÉ

Let's look at a case that shows how to reorganize your prior best work skills to give them the most attention by the reader.

Case Study

JAMILA, A FINANCE MANAGER FROM KENYA

Jamila had a journey that included international studies in London, several degrees, and experience working for others in the financial field outside the U.S. In addition, she was now running her own retail business. She wanted to get back into a corporate finance career. The first résumé she shared did not tell a story of her financial skills that would make her a desirable candidate for a corporate finance career. This happened because she used a traditional, chronological résumé in which her recent retail entrepreneurial work was showcased in detail but her previous financial and administrative skills were minimized near the bottom. To a recruiter, it would look like she was currently so involved in running her own business that she would not be motivated to fit into a structured business environment. She was shown how to revise her résumé to tell a more accurate story with an objective at the top under her contact information that emphasized her financial skills gained in both corporate and entrepreneurial work. She could then present her relevant skills first.

At first, she hesitated to make the changes to her résumé. We did not hear from her for over a month. She said her delay was due to a combination of family and work issues plus questioning whether these changes needed to be made. When the new résumé was finally ready, she resumed our plans to advance her job search.

The best structure for your résumé has your key contact information at the top. This includes your name (and nickname in quotes if you use one), phone, email address, LinkedIn profile link, and city where you live. You do not need to put your street address or zip code, as these details can cause the reader to discriminate against you based on whether they perceive your neighborhood — and therefore you — as being undesirable or not suitable for the type of job you are applying for. There can also be bias against distance. If your home is many miles from the employer, a fact that does not concern you, the hiring manager could feel it will keep you from accepting the position or cause you to be late. So, put the city, but not your specific address, at the top of your résumé.

Next, put your legal visa status in the top section under your address and email so the hiring manager or HR team understands that you are ready to work right now. Use language such as "Lawful Permanent Resident," "Green Card Holder," or "U.S. Citizen." If you do not put this on the résumé, the reader may assume that you need visa sponsorship and may not call you for an interview. If you do need visa sponsorship, then do not put anything on the résumé and deal with that in the interview process. There are ideas on how to handle this in the interview section later in this book.

After the personal information, you may want to put an area titled "Work Objective" or "Key Skills." Here and throughout your résumé, you should be using as many words as you can from the job descriptions of the jobs you want as you write about your skills, metrics for results, and accomplishments.

Your work history usually comes next, with the most recent work at the top and the older work further down. The same goes in the education section. This is called reverse chronological order, with the most recent position on top and the earlier work or schooling below. Include the city and work dates as well. You can include non-paid or volunteer work in your work history if it is meaningful to the job search and position.

Next, include a section for your education. This starts with the most recent educational program or degree first and the earlier ones below. There should be a city and date for each program or certificate. You should include any recent trainings or short courses you have done in the U.S. as well, to show your familiarity with U.S. skills and professional language in your field. If your education was over 20 years ago you may wish to omit the dates so that your training does not seem outdated.

At the end of the résumé, consider listing one to three personal interests. These should be the kinds of interests that might engage those who interview you and show that you will be a good part of a team. Good selections include fun, social activities you like, such as traveling, restaurants, golf, soccer, tennis, book clubs, or watching your local, professional sports team. Do not put solitary hobbies such as violin, piano, reading, swimming, chess, or hiking, as they are not likely to help your interview process. You can make an exception if you were truly world-class in some pursuit and can tie that into your drive for excellence, such as being the top women's chess player in your home country. That recognition would indicate strategic skills and work dedication, which are excellent skills for an interviewer to see.

Why This Works

You want the HR recruiter or the hiring manager to see that you are skilled to do the work that was described in the job description. You will need to "brag" about what you have done, which is often a bit uncomfortable for certain cultures. But, in the United States, they will expect to see some bragging in your cover letter and résumé to show that you are proud of what you have done and what you will do for your next organization. You want to make it easy for the hiring manager to see how your skills will fit the job, not make them work hard to fit your background to the job requirements. You do not want to distract the reader with irrelevant work and skills you have; instead, focus on why you will be the best candidate to accomplish the goals of the company. You have so much to offer!

Next, we will look at considerations about what name to use on the résumé and for the interview process.

WHICH NAME SHOULD YOU USE?

In the case study below, Khaliyah decided to change her name to make her job search easier.

Case Study

KHALIYAH, AN ADMINISTRATIVE ASSISTANT FROM AZERBAIJAN

Many of our international people in the United States from China, India, and other countries have a long name that is quite different than American names. One client was from Azerbaijan and had a name that many English speakers found difficult to say: Khaliyah. She started using an easier name: Katie. That name made it much easier to introduce her to one of our local companies, who invited her to a job-shadow day in their general administrative department. The shorter name also helped as she did a full job search, since company hiring managers could easily say her name.

The choice of a name is an emotional, personal, and somewhat political topic. In a perfect world, we would each use our given name or preferred name and other people would happily learn to pronounce it. But this is not a perfect world, so you need to assess options on this topic.

In the interview process, you want the interviewer to be comfortable calling you by name and introducing you to others in the hiring process. You want her to like you and to be engaged with you. If your name is hard for an American to pronounce or to say easily, you may have a choice to make.

One choice is to select an Americanized name and an email address to match. The other choice is for those with foreign names to keep their original name as a sense of pride and personal identity. This relates to a feeling of "not giving in" to the American view of names and keeping your personal family identity with your given name. In today's world, foreign-born people, or those with names from another culture, feel vulnerable and not always seen as they want to be seen. Using your given name is one way to be seen, and you may feel that is how you want to present yourself. That is understandable. But it is important to consider if this will meet your other objectives and if there may be different ways to have your given name seen and used.

One way to help with your given name is to find a nice way to share it with the interviewer, such as "The best way to say my name is as follows..." You can put a pronunciation of your name in parentheses below your name on your résumé. Or you can use an Americanized nickname that makes it easy for the interviewer to say and use that name with others in your targeted hiring organization. You can put your nickname in quotation marks after your given name on your résumé or in any written materials. For example, in the case study above, Khaliyah could put her name at the top of her résumé as Khaliyah "Katie" Abdulova. You may want to get a specific email address that uses your nickname and use that email in your job search.

If your name is not easily associated with a gender, you may want to put the pronouns below, such as "She/Her/Hers," "He/Him/His," or "They/Them/Theirs." This can make the interviewer have a better idea of whom to expect to meet.

Once hired, you can decide if you are comfortable with your nickname or if you want to start to encourage your colleagues to use your given, legal name. You will need to coach them over time and be patient. Remember that while your colleague may want to use your preferred name, they may struggle to say it. If that person struggles, they may find ways to avoid using the name in conversation. If they are not confident that they can say the name correctly, they are less likely to introduce you to others. So take some time to help them learn it.

Why This Works

In the United States, professional relationships tend to be casual and on a first-name basis. We are informal about making introductions and we like being casual. If we see someone we know from work or from the community at an event, we are likely to go over to chat with the person. This is true even if the person is in a higher-ranked position than our own. One way to increase your opportunities for connection is to make it easy for the other person to remember your name and to say your name. While it can be hurtful to you that those in the United States do not try to learn foreign names very well, it is your choice how to react. Maybe a shorter version of your given name or finding a way to make your name memorable will be your best answer.

Be aware that there is research showing there is bias in the hiring process regarding names on résumés. While progressive companies and progressive people do not want to think they are prejudiced against names that are long or difficult for them to spell or pronounce, there is evidence that hiring teams are biased toward names that are more like their own and easier for them to say. Keeping that in mind, you are the only one who can decide the best way to present your name professionally.

Now you will hear from a guest contributor who has helped many foreign-born people adjust their résumés to the American style.

EXPERT CONTRIBUTOR

Anita Barker, VP Director of Education & Training, International Institute of St. Louis

The International Institute of St. Louis (IISTL) was founded in 1919. For years, the Institute has helped clients find jobs — often a survival job, initially — so they can have income to support themselves and their families while acclimating to U.S. workplace culture. In recent years, IISTL began offering a formal training called CAIP — Career Advancement for International Professionals — a professional job search training that teaches clients the information and skills they need to conduct effective searches for professional jobs. The five-week, 16-hour training program for international professionals features:

- Writing effective résumés and cover letters
- Job interviews and professional communication

- Job search tactics and LinkedIn
- Dealing with online applications
- Recertification and credentialing resources

HERE IS OUR ADVICE:

For the résumé, the top one-third of the résumé must effectively connect to the job opening to catch the attention of a hiring manager and/or get through an applicant tracking system that may be used by the company. Just as it is for native-born applicants, another challenge for you is being able to explain your professional work experience in terms of concrete accomplishments rather than through a list of job duties. If you have had interrupted professional careers because of years in a refugee camp before coming to the U.S. or because of working in completely unrelated jobs for survival after arrival to the U.S., it is sometimes difficult for you to convey both your relevant professional experience abroad and your U.S. work experience in unrelated occupations in a way which effectively puts your work history in context. Given the reality that hiring managers spend little time reviewing individual résumés, we stress the importance of creating a résumé that gives information as clearly as possible without raising questions that can sometimes distract a hiring manager.

Keeping in mind the need to overcome these challenges, our CAIP program created a résumé sample (see Resources section). Key elements of the résumé sample include:

- Ensuring that the résumé is applicant tracking system–friendly in terms of font choice, keywords, and concise statements with zero spelling errors or typos

- For foreign names that may be difficult for a U.S. hiring manager to pronounce or remember, adding an American nickname in parenthesis

- Ensuring that your contact email is aligned with your name and easy to remember

- A statement of "U.S. Permanent Resident — no visa sponsorship needed" (or "work authorized — no visa sponsorship needed") as part of the contact information at the top of the résumé

- A professional summary statement that clearly states the type of position you are seeking and puts unrelated U.S. work experience in context

- Using English words as much as possible to help the U.S. hiring manager better understand information about degrees, businesses, universities, and cities

- For relevant work experience, conveying professional work experience using accomplishment statements and concrete details

- For unrelated work experience, limiting information of position, company and location, employment dates, and basic duties (especially duties that show an increase in responsibility)

"

After the résumé is done, you will need to develop a cover letter for each job application.

THE COVER LETTER AND YOUR SUBMITTED APPLICATION

Many job postings request that you send in a résumé but they may not mention a cover letter. A cover letter can be particularly important for the foreign-born job seeker to give the best reasons why you should be considered for a certain job. It shows your correct usage of the English language. Because this is so important, you may want to have a native English speaker proofread your cover letter before you send it to make sure your wording is correct.

The cover letter is a specific letter you create just for that organization and for that specific job. It describes why you are interested in the organization. You tell why your skills are a good match for the words that describe the job. You can highlight work you may have done in your home country before you started working in the U.S. You attach this letter to your résumé when you submit electronically.

The cover letter needs to be specific. If the company is a pet food company, you should state that your family has always had a dog and you would love to work for a company that cares about the bonds that people make with their pets. If the company makes farm equipment, you can mention something about your interest in feeding the world through farming. This connection to the mission of the organization is even more important if you are applying to a non-profit organization. The organization that works to end racism or to feed the homeless wants to know why you care about this issue. Please put this in your cover letter, along with your skills to do the work of the specific job. There is an example at the back of this book.

You will see below that the cover letter can make a big difference in your résumé and job application getting a positive response.

Case Study

MOHAMED, A WRITER FROM SYRIA

Mohamed was a writer and storyteller. He spoke English well and was very smart. When he saw a part-time job that interested him, he sent off his résumé by itself. He did not hear back from the company. When he took the time to write and attach a good cover letter that explained exactly why his skills made him a good candidate for the specific position at the company seeking a translator, he was called and ultimately started working for the organization.

A few weeks later, he saw another listing for a similar part-time job at a different organization. He wrote a good cover letter with his résumé to apply, and he asked an organization to write a recommendation for him for the position. He did not get the job and he was discouraged about the process. He was not happy that they had ignored him and not offered him an interview for the job. He did get a call after a few weeks and then was more optimistic about other positions he would apply for in the future.

The cover letter made Mohamed's total application stand out. You can do that as well. Do you need a cover letter with your résumé even if the job description just asks that you send your résumé? The answer is *yes*.

Your résumé tells a story about you and your skills, plus the kind of work you seek. It lets a hiring manager or recruiter see your past work and educational history, including any recognition you have received. It does *not* tell the hiring manager reasons you would be a great contributor to the job and why you believe you are a great fit for the organization. Those are the kinds of things you can say in your cover letter. For the actual submission online, you can make one document that has your cover letter and your résumé together. Remember, use the power of both the résumé and cover letter to make the best impression on the hiring manager so they will want to select you.

Why This Works

You want to demonstrate to your future employer that you can organize your thoughts and communicate well. You want to show the specific skills that prove you are a strong candidate. Other aspects of your résumé may not support that direction, such as gap years or less-than-optimal jobs you worked as you transitioned to the U.S. job market. So, draw attention to your more relevant strengths and take the attention away from any weaknesses that might be seen in your résumé.

Now let's discuss the importance of the people in your network.

THE IMPORTANCE OF YOUR U.S. NETWORK

After you moved to the United States, you probably became friends with others from your home country. Your spouse/partner may be going to work with a mostly American group of co-workers. Or maybe your spouse works at a company owned by friends from your home country. You may have met a few Americans in your neighborhood, in your building, or at your child's school. Yet overall, most of the people you know look and sound like you.

When you socialize with those from your home country it is comfortable. Language, food, customs, and expectations on how to behave are shared. But these friends are likely to know the same circle of people that you know. That means they know of the same new jobs in the community that you know of as well. If you want to have more chances at the growing number of jobs in your new community, you need to start making friends and relationships with people outside your first circle of friends. You need to meet new people that touch on other interests in your life, both in person and online. These are the relationships most likely to give you knowledge about new jobs you might consider applying for.

This desire to grow the circle of people you know means you need to learn the U.S. method of building relationships, called networking. You will see how networking opens you to learning about jobs that are not even posted yet for the public to see. And we will discuss how these new relationships lead to the planned way you can turn those new friendships into introductions to your possible new job.

This first case highlights how a limited network needs to be expanded to include new people.

Case Study

ELVIR, AN ACCOUNTANT FROM BOSNIA

Elvir had been in St. Louis for a year. He had a job but wanted a better one to use his skills at a higher level. He was looking for a new job and understood how many jobs are found through personal connections. He was on LinkedIn and had a fair number of network connections. But on a closer review, his connections were mostly from the Bosnian community. While that is good, it did not open him up to more job connections. He evaluated other people he knew but had not yet invited to join his LinkedIn network. He made notes of the parents of his children's friends that he knew from the school parent-teacher organization (PTO) and from birthday parties. He listed names from his soccer network, none of whom he had yet invited into his LinkedIn contacts.

This second case shows how connections can multiply once you start meeting more people.

Case Study

MILANA, AN ADVERTISING ACCOUNT EXECUTIVE FROM CHILE

Milana had worked for an international advertising agency in her home country. She was struggling to find a job in the U.S. Though the St. Louis Mosaic Project Professional Connector Program, she was introduced to the head of a growing digital agency in town. The agency owner had many connections she shared with Milana. Milana soon got an offer through that network.

Because Milana is a natural connector, not only did she accept the job offer, she also became an excellent connector for others. Always smiling and happy to those she knows or those who are new to her, Milana is one of those who got helped and now is excelling professionally. She is happy in her job and her new role of helping others.

You may hate the word "networking." It brings up images of stiff conversations at boring events and forced situations. Instead, think about building relationships. You decide that you want to make new relationships that will bring personal and professional benefits to you and to others. By making these relationships, you open yourself up for others to create opportunities that are best for you. Sometimes employers may even shape a job or write a posted job description that has all your skills if the hiring manager has met you at a networking event and wants you to be the person in the job.

Keep a positive attitude about building new relationships. Set up your own plan. One way to do this is that when you attend an event, either a professional event or a social or sporting event, set a goal of making three good, new relationships. Seek out people to talk with who look interesting to you or who are sitting near you. Ask questions about them — about their family, what they like to do, or why they like the event you are attending. When the person asks about you, share some positive things about yourself and why you like the event you are attending. You can mention that you are "in transition" in your job search, which is a polite way to say you are unemployed. You can say that you are seeking a position to do accounting, financial analysis, data analytics, customer service, lab sciences, or whatever you are aiming for. Ask for the person's business card if possible. Give them yours. You might say "I look forward to staying in touch." After you step away from the person, make a mental or written note about their name so you can follow up.

The next day, send the person a LinkedIn invitation with a personalized comment that says, "It was great to meet you at the event yesterday." There is a good chance the other person will accept your invitation to connect if you personalize it. If they do not accept, just realize that they were busy. Move on. There are many people who will accept, and that is all that matters.

The power of building an informal network of U.S. friends as well as a LinkedIn network of U.S. friends comes over time. It is like investing savings for the future: You invest your time into relationships for your future. If you see a job posted at a company where a friend works, you can then ask your friend about the job. You can post information about your interests and thoughts on work topics on LinkedIn and tag people in the companies for which you would like to work. They may connect with you after that. All of this happens before you are active in the search for a new job. It positions you as someone well-connected with a good network in the field. Show that you are engaged in your work field by building a network of connections to others in that field.

Why This Works

You are in control of your network. You bring value to those you meet. For these reasons, you will find yourself invited and connected with many more people once you break out of your current circle. Americans are open to adding new people to their circles because they, too, want to enlarge their own networks for their personal and professional benefits. You offer a great new gateway to new ideas for those you meet. Native-born people are often open and curious to add new friends and professional connections. This is a good time in American society as more people want to add diverse friendships to their relationships and knowledge.

Here is some information from a woman who is known to be well-connected to others. You can learn from her immigrant story and successful career.

EXPERT CONTRIBUTOR

Susanne Evens, Founder & CEO, AAA Translation

In the summer of 1992, my family and I made the decision to create a life in St. Louis, Missouri. My husband (at the time), my two daughters, and I lived in my mother-in-law's picturesque two-bedroom home until we found a house to call our home. Making the decision to leave my homeland, Germany, was equal parts excitement and terror. When the decision was made, what followed quickly was action — not a well-researched plan with tactics.

With an international business degree and a degree as a foreign language correspondent from Germany and knowledge of five languages, I thought it would be easy to find a position with a firm that could use my international experience. I started sending out résumés and calling prospective employers; however, these actions were unsuccessful.

I quickly learned that other actions were needed to capture the attention of hiring managers to secure an interview.

Through a family connection, I was able to launch my career in the U.S.

Eight years later, when I decided to launch my own company, AAA Translation, I began to attend many networking events.

A few facts to keep in mind when launching your networking plan: The average American is not used to dealing with foreigners. About 60% of Americans do not have a passport. With the exceptions of some large cities and tourist areas, most citizens do not find many opportunities to interact with outsiders, and their knowledge of other cultures is limited.

Therefore, researching local culture, customs, and the companies you wish to meet is of utmost importance.

Here are a few tips to help you make the most out of a networking opportunity:

- Smile genuinely. A smile humanizes you and makes you more approachable. In networking, that is extremely important. Plus, smiling improves your appearance, creates trust and rapport, and overall helps you and the others around you feel good. And in networking, smiling shows that you are open to conversation.

- Listen actively. Encourage the other person to talk about themself. The easiest way to become a good conversationalist is to know how to listen. What do they enjoy? Hobbies? Travels? Be careful with the topic of sports unless it is a sport that you both enjoy.

- Remember names. My tricks: When I meet someone new, I repeat their name in my mind at least five times and write it in my little black book that goes with me everywhere, or I put it on the business card I received from them. If there is something very distinct about them, I note that too. An immediate follow-up with someone you really enjoyed meeting via e-mail or a handwritten notecard is highly recommended.

- Make the other person feel important and do it sincerely.

You will find that Americans like to sell themselves in any dialogue, due to the entrepreneurial spirit in American culture. The American educational system encourages public presentations, which was totally foreign to me in the beginning.

What worked best for me was to get involved in my community. It started with a German street festival where I saw the St. Louis–Stuttgart Sister Cities booth. I started volunteering for the organization in various capacities and have been the president since 2006.

By volunteering for organizations that align with your interests, not only can you learn new things, you can also gain connections that are priceless. By being the president of our local Stuttgart Sister Cites organization, I had the pleasure of traveling with several of our mayors to my hometown area of Stuttgart and introducing them to my culture and trade opportunities there.

MORE TIPS:

1. Connect with cultural organizations and volunteer to help.
2. Research local and global chambers of commerce for people and meetings.
3. Contact the honorary consul of your home country for networking events.
4. Join a professional association specific to your career.
5. Attend global festivals, job fairs, or workshops, and join online Meetup groups or attend book clubs and other groups aligned with your interests.

NOW, LET'S DISCUSS VIRTUAL NETWORKING:

LinkedIn can be a central element in an effective networking strategy. Make sure to keep your profile updated.

Join special interest groups on Facebook and follow industry experts on Twitter.

ESPECIALLY IMPORTANT:

Practice your "elevator pitch," meaning your short and positive introduction. For example, mine is "Hello, my name is Susanne Evens, I am the founder and CEO of AAA Translation, and originally from Germany. What is your favorite country?"

Happy Networking!

>

In the next segment, we will talk about how some jobs are never posted but get filled through the networks of current employees. You can use this to your advantage as you expand your network of new people in your life.

THE ROLE OF NETWORKING VS. POSTED JOB OPPORTUNITIES

Here are examples of jobs that were created because a company saw talent in the international candidate after they were introduced to the candidate through their current employee but before a job had been posted.

Case Studies

ZEHRA, AN ENGINEER FROM TURKEY

Zehra met company leaders when she was applying for a job. That job opportunity did not work out for her, but the company manager and Zehra kept in touch. Several weeks later, they called to say that they had some new business and were creating a job that would be perfect for her, and they asked if she could come back in to talk about it. She now works on the company's largest account. They never posted the job she was offered — it happened because she made a good impression and kept in touch in a positive way.

Zehra had many questions about the U.S. working environment. She kept in close contact with mentors about the customs of the workplace, the right attire for the workplace, the best ways to connect with her new work colleagues, and the right way to ask for some flexibility in her days off. She was very "coachable" and open to new ideas on how to do things a new way to be successful in a mid-size U.S. company.

> ### HIEN, A MANAGER FROM VIETNAM
>
> *Hien was extremely outgoing. He had many friends in the Vietnamese community but also had friends from many other international communities. Whenever there was an event after work, he showed up. He made it a point to make new relationships everywhere he went. When he needed a new job, he had contacts at most of the companies in the region and friends went out of their way to make introductions for him to new people at their companies.*

In the first case study, Zehra made a positive impression when she did an initial interview, and that starting relationship led to a future offer. In the second case, Hien developed many friendships through his networking that ultimately opened job opportunities for him when those friends made personal introductions for him. Both did a good job adding to their networks.

Why This Works

"Posted" jobs are visible to the public. These are posted on jobs boards, social media, or the company website. In many industries, there are also "unposted" jobs whose job descriptions for upcoming positions have not yet been fully written but are still in the process of being approved. These are jobs you may not know about unless someone inside the company knows about them and tells you. They are sometimes called "the hidden job market."

Sometimes, you will see a job posted on a company website or a jobs website and want to hear more about it from someone who works in the company before you apply. Or you may hear of an unposted opportunity that is being considered at a company you are interested in and want to learn more. If you are looking for a new job, you want to hear of all these opportunities! The best way to do this is to build a broad network of community connections before you need or want to look for a new job. That means the time is now to start building your network!

In the next segment, we will talk about how your growing network of connections will help people make "warm introductions" for you to possible new job opportunities.

THE "WARM INTRODUCTION"

In this case study, we see how a candidate benefited from a personal introduction or "warm introduction" to a person with new company opportunities.

Case Study

CHENG, A GENERAL MANAGER FROM CHINA

A very accomplished manager, Cheng shared his background with his mentor. He had many skills, as he spoke four languages, had worked for government and business employers, and was highly intelligent. A company needed a supervisor and business planner. This company had workers from several countries who spoke languages that Cheng also spoke, and the company was growing, so a person who could take on more tasks over time would be an asset. A mutual friend of this candidate introduced him to the owner of the growing company with a personal recommendation. They met, and he received a job offer the next week. He started the following week. If he had sent his résumé through the regular application channels, it is less likely he would have received the job offer.

Cheng was very resourceful. When his first job ended due to the company's business issues, he made more connections and quickly got offered another position at a different company. He has a versatile personality and knows how to shift his skills. He showed a flexible nature that was apparent when the new company spoke with him. Networking and flexibility are good traits in a time of big changes in our world.

Many of the international people who come to the U.S. have a big network of people they know in their own ethnic community. While this is great for the social side of fitting in to a new community, it does not help with networking or getting a "warm introduction" to a potential employer. A "warm introduction" is when a person knows you and the employer or hiring manager and can put in a personal good word about you. That person will write or call the hiring person and say "I know a great candidate for your position. She just applied. She would be a good fit. You know our region wants to attract and retain diverse talent in our community. Can I encourage you to include her in your first round of interviews?" This is the opposite of a "cold call," when you call a company or person without an introduction.

You can ask someone you know to make a warm introduction to an employee in your desired company or to the person who is hiring for a specific job. Sometimes that person will agree to make the introduction. Sometimes the person will not, as they are not comfortable doing so. A nice way to ask is to say "I saw that there is a position posted that fits my skills. I have applied already. The exact position is X. I am attaching my résumé and believe that my background would be a good fit. Would you be comfortable making an introduction for me? Could you ask that I be in the first round of interviews?" If the person declines, thank them for reviewing your information and tell them you will find another way to connect with the company.

The first round of interviews is often done through a series of phone or video screening calls by a recruiter. The best candidates make it to the second round. Asking if you can get into the first round of interviews is not too much to ask of someone you know because it is a personal appeal. This "warm introduction" can make the difference if there are over 100 applicants and the company will narrow that to 10 to 15 candidates for a first round of phone or video calls to screen candidates. The goal will be to identify a final few candidates for the hiring manager to meet for a personal interview and decision.

Why This Works

In most job fields, there is a preference for hiring employees who are known to the people in the field. This works in favor of those who have lived in the community for a long time and have done good networking to build industry relationships personally. But when someone has moved internationally, they do not have those connections, so they must be built. The more you can attend events in your field and make personal connections, the more likely you will meet someone who can tell you of a possible job that has not been posted yet or make a warm introduction for you to a potential employer.

If someone in the company puts in a good word about knowing you, you become more attractive to the company. It means that the person in the company thinks highly of you and believes you would add to the organization's goals. If your résumé lists your foreign university and foreign company references, having this local recommendation could mean a great deal as it shows you are comfortable being with American people and are familiar with U.S. business operations.

Now, you understand more about what is meant by the warm introduction. As you advance in your job search skills, let's look more deeply at how you build your professional connections.

USING LINKEDIN AND OTHER PROFESSIONAL NETWORKS

This section shows the path between LinkedIn and the professional network in your field to find a job. Let's look at two case studies of people who did this in different ways.

Case Studies

JULIANA, AN ENGINEER FROM BRAZIL

Juliana had been looking for a job for several months. Her LinkedIn profile was strong, showing her educational and work experiences. She used Indeed and LinkedIn to seek out relevant positions as they were posted. And sometimes when a friend would see a relevant job posted on LinkedIn, she would put Juliana's name in the comments section online so Juliana would be alerted. That way Juliana could immediately look at the position. The company might also note Juliana's name and check out her profile on the site. This all happened smoothly and quickly due to the power of LinkedIn. Juliana made several good job connections this way that led to meetings and interviews.

NOK, AN ACCOUNTANT FROM THAILAND

Nok was actively job hunting. She attended many professional events. She was active in two Asian organizations. She signed up for accounting seminars. She offered to be a presenter. She was outgoing and made several good connections at each event. Nok exhibited positive energy; her personality was a real advantage. She was eventually hired by a mid-size accounting firm and is doing well there.

For Juliana, people in her professional network could easily identify new job opportunities for her just by putting her name into online sites like LinkedIn. In Nok's case, she personally showed up at events to use her professional networks on an in-person basis that boosted her job opportunities.

LinkedIn makes the job searching process speed along. Sometimes it is too fast to process in your head! But today's job world happens online on LinkedIn, Indeed, and other sites. If you can manage that flow of information, it will work to your advantage as it did for Juliana.

LinkedIn allows you to put in the name of a company in your city and see all the people who work there. This allows you to find the right person to connect with or to contact with a question about the operations of the company. You can type in your university and your city to find anyone with that combination who might have connections to assist your search. As you build your network and connect to people on LinkedIn, you can easily see if someone you know has connections at a company with an open job that interests you.

It is important that you fill out a complete and professional LinkedIn profile. In the most basic profile, you need a professional appearing photo at the top of your LinkedIn profile, not one with a cap on your head or a sporty shirt. For LinkedIn, do not use a casual shot where you are in a sleeveless blouse or dramatic scarf. You do not need to be wearing a suit and tie or blazer, but you should wear a solid-color top with your best smile toward the viewer. You need to fill in the right keywords under your work description and in your objectives section. You need to be posting comments on postings by other people in your field. You should post a good story about your professional interests every week or so. You can write an article and put in the name of others you know who can read and comment on it. This is where career recruiters look to see your profile and whether you appear to be keeping up with your field. This is especially important as an international job seeker. You want to show that your English is strong and that you are connected to your career field.

It is awkward to make LinkedIn requests to people you feel you hardly know. What if they ignore or deny your requests? You may be worried and unsure of yourself. That is totally normal. Even native-born people feel a sense of vulnerability when they think about making LinkedIn invitations. The best way to get others to accept your online request to connect is to personalize the invitation by stating how you know each other and that you look forward to connecting. It gives you the option to "put a personalized note" when you start to make a connection request, and you should always do this. Do not just push the "Send" button without a greeting. Say something like "It was good to see you at the Engineer Club monthly meeting. I look forward to connecting." Most people will accept if you put a personalized note. You can try it and see! You should get acceptances over half the time if you make that personalization. And this larger network is the best way to open yourself up to more jobs. Remember that connections work both ways — if someone agrees to connect with you, then they will benefit in the future from knowing you. When you find a job and have a larger network, you will be able to assist others who seek introductions and connections.

Organizations that involve your ethnicity or your professional skills are great places to meet people in person and through LinkedIn. There are local groups such as chapters of the American Marketing Association and Engineering Clubs. There are chapters of legal and accounting organizations. There are Hispanic, Asian, and African chambers of commerce, plus business groups from all different nationalities. There are gatherings in person and online for local job seekers and recruiters needing talent. These are all filled with people who have shared interests with you and who will want you to be successful. The best advice: Be there! By being present, you indicate your interest and your relationship skills. You show your motivation and drive. You will find the groups to be very welcoming to you. It is a fun and natural way to gain professional and personal connections.

Why This Works

Finding a job and building a career require relationships. That is what LinkedIn and professional organizations provide. They represent positive ways to find people and to invite them to connect with you. Your job opportunities grow through the network of your connections, so there is power in this for your job search and for future career growth. You will be pleasantly surprised — you may even find it enjoyable! There is an additional section for advanced LinkedIn usage beginning on page 171.

How about a few confidence boosters for your job search? Here are some ideas that will add to the way you present yourself in the process.

BUSINESS CARDS AND OTHER PROFESSIONAL MATERIALS

How can you look the most professional and confident as you go through the stages of the job-hiring process? There are several suggestions below that will boost your confidence.

Case Study

ALEXANDRIA, A MANAGER FROM EGYPT

Alexandria went into an office for an informational interview to learn more about an organization of interest to her career goals. She set her purse down on the floor and leaned in to have the discussion. She and the interviewer had a good talk, and she had a few questions to ask. When the interviewer asked her for a résumé to share with a colleague in the office nearby, she did not have one with her. As they proceeded in the discussion, she had nowhere to make any notes when the interviewer gave her some organizations to contact. The interviewer offered her some paper and a pen, which she took gratefully. She did not have a business card to hand out. Lastly, she asked only three questions. She was anxious and embarrassed to not feel prepared with the right materials or questions.

To make matters worse, in the days following the interview, she sent a thank you note written on lined school paper, which gave a poor impression to the interviewer.

You can see that Alexandria was not very prepared for the discussion.

You want to be able to hand out a business card when you attend an event. This is true whether you are working in business, have your own company, are a student, or are not working outside the home at the moment. You want a simple business card that has your name, email, cell phone, possibly LinkedIn address, and one or two lines about yourself. These lines can contain the specialty that you want the person to remember, such as "Digital Content Creator," "Mechanical Engineer," or "Senior Accountant." If you have a card from the company you work for, that may suffice. Or you may prefer to have a separate, personal card created so you can give them out when you do not need to put your employer forward or do not have a current employer.

It is recommended that when you order your cards, such as from VistaPrint or Moo, you also order notecards with envelopes. That way you can keep a few notecards in your portfolio or computer cover, and after you meet with someone you can quickly write a personal thank you or appreciation comment. You should certainly send an email thank-you. Still, it is impactful when someone receives a handwritten card with thanks for the time spent together. You can thank the person you met for coffee or that you spoke with at a reception. It makes a big impression!

It is a good idea to buy a nice portfolio folder that is about 10"×13" or so, with a notepad inside plus space to hold printed, clean copies of your résumé. This portfolio case can be textured or a plastic leather imitation. You will be surprised how many times you use this. You may take it to your interviews and to meetings to take notes. You will look and feel like a professional. Put a pen inside. Put three copies of your résumé inside. Put any flat "show and tell" from your prior work experience, such as drawings, a newsletter you created, a printout of a website you designed, or a menu from the restaurant where you worked. You can also bring materials from your research about the organization you are visiting:

brochures, online materials, consumer reviews, or competition printouts for discussion. This will give you things to touch and share in the interview, which will build your confidence. And if you aren't fully comfortable speaking English, your interview will flow better when the discussion has some "show and tell" about you or about the company that you bring to discuss. Let your enthusiasm be visible as you share any materials you have in your portfolio folder.

Why This Works

Confidence is especially important. When you look prepared, you will have confidence. The interviewers will see how you have put yourself together. They will be pleased to be handed a fresh résumé if they ask. They will see that you have written down good questions in advance on your nice notepad. With all your materials in one place, you will be organized and professional in your presentation.

SUMMARY OF STAGE II
Pre-Job Interview Tools and Tips

1. Develop the right résumé and online presence.

2. Use a well-written cover letter to draw attention to your specific skills and interest in that organization when you apply for a job.

3. Build a network of personal relationships beyond the community from your home country.

4. Determine if someone in your network can inform you of job openings that may be upcoming.

5. Ask a person in your network to make a "warm introduction" for you if you see that the person is connected to a position or company in which you have an interest.

6. Join several professional organizations to enhance your network of connections and use LinkedIn to add to those relationships.

7. Order business cards and a portfolio so you have the right professional materials that enhance your personal appearance.

Next, we will talk about the different interview stages. This will include the pre-interview screening, possible interviews with HR professionals, and then interviews with the actual hiring manager, plus others. This knowledge will make the U.S. process easier to understand for your planning and practicing.

USE THIS SPACE TO TAKE NOTES *about preparing for interviews. You may want to review online résumés and note keywords for your field, list people you know through community activities you can add to your network, research what professional organizations are available in your industry, and note the kinds of business cards that appeal to you.*

STAGE III

Interview Processes and Preparation

It takes thoughtful attention to get ready for your interview process. There are things to consider before you get into the actual interview, such as the structure of the interview process and who will be doing the interviews. You need to be set up for video interviews. You need to understand the most likely types of interviews that you will encounter so you are confident and ready. Let's talk about how you can do a great job in the process!

The American interview system has become more complicated in recent years due to technology for online application questions and the professional input on candidate testing from human resources professionals. Human resources professionals are often called the HR team, which can be inside an organization or hired as outside contractors. These people work with hiring technology to evaluate the hundreds of résumés and cover letters that may come in for a posted job. Your first and ongoing contact with the company is likely to be through that person or team, ether inside or outside the company itself.

Technology allows the application process to include online tests and tracking of your application process. Human resources professionals inside or outside a company now do much of the interview work before you get a chance to interview with the person you will ultimately report to, the hiring manager. Make that HR professional your friend!

Case Study:

IRINA, A MANAGER FROM RUSSIA

After applying to dozens of jobs, Irina got a response from the HR person at a good company of interest. The HR person scheduled a pre-interview screening, a phone interview, with Irina. This first phone interview discussed Irina's background, skills, and general fit for the role. The HR person then asked Irina what her salary expectation was for the job.

Her salary had been high in her home country, but this was a different country in which her skills may be used differently. She did not want to say a salary number that was so high that she would not be invited to continue in the job interview process, but she also did not want to suggest a salary that was too low.

Being prepared, Irina had done research on different job websites to know the range that this kind of work typically was paid, and she said, "I am looking to be paid in the range of $55,000 to $65,000 annually, plus benefits." The HR person stated that the position being discussed was in the low end of that range and asked if that was still acceptable to Irina. The discussion continued and Irina was invited to proceed to additional rounds of interviews with the actual hiring manager.

This example showed how pre-screening is used. Let's see how the pre-screening fits into the full interview process.

INTERVIEW TYPES: PRE-INTERVIEW SCREENING, ONE-PERSON INTERVIEWS AND PANEL INTERVIEWS

You may experience several kinds of interviews for one job at one company. Your first contact might be a pre-interview screening call to determine if you have the right overall skills and salary expectations. This could be followed by additional interviews that may involve one person or up to four people together in an interview with you. Having multiple people interview you together is called a panel interview format.

PRE-INTERVIEW SCREENING INTERVIEW

Pre-interview screening is intended to pre-qualify you for the position. It is used to determine if you are a good enough candidate to meet the actual hiring manager. Some companies do this by phone, and some do it by video call. They may want to check out your background, degrees, or skills. The interviewer wants to know if you are in the right salary range, as was described in the case of Irina. The HR person is usually the one to put the question to you about what your prior salary was or what your salary expectation is today.

When U.S. jobs are posted, they usually do not list a salary range. It would be much easier for you as a potential candidate if posted jobs did list a salary range. Some more progressive companies are posting the salary for a given job, to ensure that the right expectations are known by applicants. This means that you must do work online *in advance* of the call to understand the level of work you believe is the right level for you and what that job salary range might be. Then, you need to judge if a posted job fits that range. Websites like **www.salary.com** and **www.glassdoor.com** have useful information of this type.

It is the job of the outside recruiter or inside human resources person to assess the fit of the applicant to the job, to see if the salary expectations are aligned with what the job pays, and to determine the personal "fit" with the company.

Coming from another country, your job may have had a salary that is relatively higher or lower than how that job is valued in the U.S. Plus, you may not have exactly all the skills needed for the U.S. job market right at the outset. Be prepared for this part of the pre-screening process with an idea of your salary goal and how to communicate that to the interviewer. After doing your research and defining your possible salary range for the job, practice communicating that. You can use Irina's example for an idea of what to say.

Why This Works

A job is evaluated for a certain pay level based on the work described and the need to fill that role. The salary is not necessarily set based on years of experience or your prior job's salary. It is a delicate discussion between the potential employer and you, the potential candidate. In that very first discussion, the HR person (or outside company who does the screening interview) wants to see if your salary expectations are close to the job's salary reality. A company does not want to spend time talking to you if your expectation is to be paid higher than what the company plans to offer. Additionally, if you value your own skills too low for their range, they may perceive that you do not have all the necessary skills or experience to correctly fill the job description. Getting close to the right number is key in that first pre-interview screening interview. After that hurdle is passed, then the next official interview with the hiring manager or a panel of interviewers discussing your possibility as the right fit for the actual job will be scheduled.

ONE INTERVIEWER OR A PANEL OF INTERVIEWERS

Your research may show that the company typically has one person interview you at a time. Or, your research may show that a company likes to have a panel of interviewers, meaning two, three, or four people who interview you at the same time. When you are invited to interview after the pre-interview screening, ask if it is possible to know the names of those you will speak with in advance. That way you can do an online search to know each person's background. It will give you insights into shared educational backgrounds or personal interests you might mention to a person during the interview process.

When you plan for the interview, remember that it is important to give each interviewer the ability to ask you a question. Then you should take the right amount of time to answer his question. Do not talk just to the person you believe is the highest ranked, as that is not how American companies want you to behave. They want to see your short and respectful answers to each person who poses a question. Have direct eye contact when you answer. Smile occasionally as well, which will relax you and make you appear more comfortable with the process. Let your personality show through! Those interviewing you want to see you as a whole person, both your skills and your working style.

Let's look at the different types of interviews you may experience when you meet the hiring manager.

Case Study:

AMUN, AN ACCOUNTING MANAGER FROM EGYPT

Amun called to discuss an interview he had just finished. He was telling the interviewer about his many different experiences over the years, but she kept asking him to go more in depth on specific projects. As he finished a project description and tried to get back to his work history, the interviewer kept asking more detailed questions about the original project he described. What was going on? Would he ever get to tell her all his good work history and how it related to the job for which he was applying?

Amun's work in his home country was most like the job he was seeking. When he arrived in the U.S., he had taken a lower-level job to pay the bills. His most recent job in the U.S. was at a much lower level. So he started to give examples of what he had accomplished in his professional work in Egypt, and that made all the difference. He told his story strongly and did well. He was invited to the next interview step.

INTERVIEW TYPES: CHRONOLOGICAL AND BEHAVIORAL

Let's discuss the chronological and behavioral interview styles you may experience. The more you know in advance and can quickly adapt to the interview style, the better job you will do in the interview itself.

There are several types of interview formats. In the U.S., there are two main interview types: chronological and behavioral. You may be most familiar with the straight chronological interview, which walks through your life and work from the past to the present. The behavioral interview is different, going into detail about what you did in different situations.

In a chronological interview, you are expected to quickly summarize your résumé. You should give a few sentences about your earliest work experience and then a few sentences about each of your other work experiences. The last one you discuss is your most recent work experience. In each case, you should try to link your prior work skills to those needed in the job for which you are interviewing. Like many foreign-born people, you might have a work gap due to moving or earlier lack of a work visa. Or you may have taken a lower-level or hourly job, sometimes called a "survival job." You can calmly explain why your recent work experience had to be different than what the interviewer might expect. Your interviewer will most likely be understanding that you did what you had to do on your path to the right level of work. In fact, many interviewers will be impressed by your strong work motivation.

It takes practice to tell your story in a comfortable way. You need to highlight the longer, past work experience that is relevant to the job for which you applied. Then, you must recognize and lightly reference the more recent work that you took to get by in your first years in the United States or when you were in a transition mode. While the work may not be related to the job you are applying for, your desire to work hard will shine through by showing that you did work even if it was not in your field. You need to direct your conversation back to your true training and related work experience for the job you are seeking in the interview. Lastly, you should practice a strong sentence to end your discussion about your most relevant skill set.

In a behavioral interview, the interviewer has read your chronological résumé from your earlier jobs to the most recent near the top. Because they think they understand your work history, they do not want to spend the interview time on that topic. Instead, what they want to do is get you talking about a key project you accomplished. After you describe the project, they will ask more questions to understand the details of your work. They may ask how you did the project, why you did it, what went well, and what did not go well. Sometimes it feels like just when you think you are done with the answer to a question, the interviewer asks for more details, such as "Why did you say that?," "Why did you do that?," or "Tell me more about that process."

The goal of this kind of interview is for the interviewer to get a better understanding of what you did for a segment of your work and really push more to see how you did the work. The interviewer may also want to understand how you were part of a team or if you were an individual contributor. Teamwork can be more important in the American workplace than in your home country. Why would this behavioral type of interview be more common now than in the past?

Well, there have been times when an interviewer was fooled by a candidate who talked about her work history in a positive way but then, after she started working, she was not able to do the skill required of the work. This more detailed interview style should prevent this kind of hiring mistake on the part of both the organization and the candidate.

If you want to learn more about behavioral interviews, look up the different kinds of behavioral interview techniques. One popular behavioral method is the STAR interview skill methodology. STAR stands for situation, task, action, and results. If you read about this kind of interview, you will be ready to notice it quickly when the interviewer asks you to give more details. You will be ready with the kind of examples from your prior work that will be needed to convey your true work activities. You will undoubtedly have wonderful work experiences that you can build upon to show your best ability. Practice telling your work story and examples in detail to a friend or family member in advance so you can do this smoothly.

You can often find out what kind of interview to expect by doing an online search about the company's interview process or by talking to a current employee you connected with through LinkedIn. This will make you better prepared. Even if you do not know what interview style will be used in advance, if you understand why the interviewer suddenly goes into more detail, you will be prepared to go into that deeper discussion. You can say to yourself, "Aha, the interviewer is moving into a behavioral interview style. I know what to say!"

When you look online about the organization or talk to current employees of the company, you will also learn if the organization is likely to use a video interview or phone interview at the beginning of the process. You can learn about the usual work clothing style and whether it is more formal or casual. This will help you prepare for the real interview. There may also be an online skill or personality test to take before you are offered the actual interview.

Many interviews are now done by video. There are online resources that can give you advice on how to look your best on video. This takes planning on your part. Have a neutral background and have your camera at eye level so you are looking right into it — do not have the camera angled up at your chin. Get a good standing light to put in front of your computer monitor or have a clip-on camera on your computer monitor so there is good light on your face. Be sure your location is quiet during the interview. If you are in a tight space, you may consider buying a three-panel screen you can set up behind you that will hide your bedroom or other personal space. You can tape your notes up on the top edge of your computer monitor so you can be looking into the camera as you see your notes.

You should prepare four to eight good questions to ask during your interview. Those can also be taped up on the upper edge of your computer monitor or written on a nice notepad if you are planning for an in-person interview. This is all part of your interview preparation.

If you are doing an interview in person, plan your appearance carefully. Be sure to shower and do not use perfume or cologne. Also, if you are a smoker, try not to smoke that day before you go. Many workplaces are non-smoking or have an outside area for smokers to use. Smoking is not common in the workplace and is not viewed positively. If the interview takes place at a restaurant, order something easy to eat and just eat a little bit so you can talk more easily. This is not the time for a spaghetti dinner!

Why This Works

The interview process is developed uniquely by each company. You goal is to make it through the early stages and get in front of the hiring manager.

To summarize: If you pass the first pre-screen interview, you may have multiple rounds of interviews to come. It is not uncommon to have four or more further interview steps, sometimes with one interviewer and sometimes up to four in the room or on the video screen with you. In each case, each step shows that you are moving forward, which is a good thing.

You may find it makes you anxious or worried to have so many rounds of interviews. Keep your calm and positive style! Remember to smile! The process will be successful if you understand the kind of interview that is being put before you.

To give you some additional tips, the next section highlights the interview skills you are most likely to be quizzed on during the interview process.

INTERVIEW COMPONENTS THAT ARE MOST IMPORTANT IN THE U.S.

We now have a chance to look at the most valued components in the U.S. marketplace.

Case Study:

BAO, A PRODUCTION MANAGEMENT SPECIALIST FROM CHINA

Bao was changing jobs. He had a series of interviews with a potential new employer where he was interested in continuing his career for greater future salary growth. As part of his preparation, he looked at the company's revenue and profit trends. He evaluated the market segment trends from public data. He looked at several new ideas that would build on areas already growing and one idea to assist a division that was declining. The potential employer was impressed with his motivation, his analytic ability, and his ability to bring new thinking to their business strategy.

This employer had a multi-interview process — four rounds of interviews, in fact. They had many steps and then many weeks with nothing happening to move the position ahead. It took a lot of patience for Bao to understand that he would be staying at his current employer longer than he thought. Bao kept up strong communications with the HR person and the hiring manager at the new company as the months proceeded with no offer. The new company kept telling him he was a perfect fit and to please be patient in the process. He was patient, and eventually the right job offer came to him.

In Bao's case, his strong presentation upfront and his calm style during the long wait had a good ending when he joined the new company. But it was the skills he demonstrated in the interview that made the company want to hire Bao. How can you prepare that way?

American companies want a candidate who shows the appropriate skill level for the position and who puts forward a positive and engaging attitude. Let's evaluate how to prepare and practice the best skills.

SKILLS

Think about the skills you offer that fit the job posted. Are they physical skills, writing skills, or analytical skills? Read about the company and see if you can judge what they value in their employees. Look at LinkedIn profiles of current employees. What can you learn from the backgrounds and job titles of the people who work there? If there is a key skill the organization stresses and you have that skill, can you bring an example of it to the interview? If it is analytics, bring an analysis you did in a previous role. If the company is talking about the needed growth trends, bring an article you read or an idea you have for a trend that will be good for the company's future. Share your thinking and show that you have the right skills for the company over the long term.

ATTITUDE

Companies say they are hiring for skills, but they are also hiring for attitude. The American positive interview attitude is open and upbeat. You will want to have stories about successes in your past and a story or two of experiences where you could have improved on a project or outcome. You may be asked about your "weakness" or "a past failure." Have two of these "weaknesses" already figured out — maybe you took on too much of the work of a team project to the exclusion of others on the team or you tend to take on too many projects and get stressed for time. It should be an acceptable weakness, not a weakness that would show you as unqualified.

You need to brag a bit about your strengths and successes, which is often hard for international applicants who come from cultures that praise a more humble approach. In addition, some home country cultures encourage a person to talk about "the team" that worked on a project and not to talk about your own personal contribution. For the United States, teamwork is important to mention. Equally important is to tell what you did uniquely, to proudly talk about your work contributions. Look the interviewer in the eye and say, "I contributed the background research portion of the project due to my strong research skills," or whatever your top skill might be.

Why This Works

The American interview blends modesty with boldness. You need to engage the interviewer about your strengths. You want to show you are a team player but also that you are committed to getting your portion of the work done in an excellent way. You may be out of your comfort zone when you brag a bit about your prior accomplishments, but the interviewer will expect you to have pride in your unique work contributions. Brag a bit!

Let's look at another approach to the interview, one in which you bring some materials to show prior work to the interviewer. This can highlight your skills as well as show how your prior work can translate into a good fit in the United States workplace. Show your great work if you have it!

Case Study:

FRANCISCO, A MARKETING MANAGER FROM NICARAGUA

Francisco was looking to leverage his work skills from Nicaragua in a slightly different industry in the United States. He had a range of work experiences but was unsure how to present the best outlook for his future with different companies. He was talkative and had done good projects in his past. He had not thought to do a "show and tell" of a marketing plan he had put together for a new target segment at a prior employer. His mentor advised that he put together a visual portfolio of his work. He also had developed some marketing material visuals that he was ready to share in the interview.

When Francisco had his interview, he showed his work. He smiled and was enthusiastic because he could point to his projects. He could brag a bit about how the work looked and how well the program performed. He shared metrics and results. While his English language skills were not perfect, his future employer could see how Francisco could do this type of work for the new organization and was impressed. Francisco showed confidence and his future employer was able to envision Francisco in the role.

If you can create some materials that show your past results or skills, please do so. Take them in a portfolio or binder and be ready to share so that your interviewer can get more insight into your strengths and how you would perform once in the workplace.

In summary, the steps are as follows to prepare for a good interview:

1. Research the company on the internet. If you know the names of the people interviewing you, do a search and LinkedIn review so you know a bit more about the person — maybe you share a skill or training. Or you might know someone in common you can ask in advance for advice about your interviewer's skills and personality.

2. Try to "experience" the company so you can talk about it as if you are already an employee — if you are interviewing with a rental car company, go online and try to rent from three companies so you can talk the differences. If you are interviewing with a beverage company, go to several stores and places the product is served and see how it is priced and served versus competition. If the company has a product or service, get five people you know who use the product or service to give you their opinions. Make notes on the strengths and weaknesses of the company's products and think of three good questions about the offerings. Why are they priced higher/lower than competitors?

What is the newest product? How was the service presented by the seller and why?

3. Use your attractive brown plastic or leather portfolio that has lined paper and a place to put some papers. You will take this with you to the interview and look organized. Have good questions written down in advance, such as more about the role, how others have progressed, what a typical day looks like, or what the key traits are that make someone successful.

4. As you meet each person, make direct eye contact. Use a firm handshake or whatever greeting is appropriate at the time. If you are on a video interview, tape your notes on a small piece of paper at the top of your screen so you are looking into the camera as you talk with good eye contact.

5. When you interview in person, bring three clean copies of your résumé in the portfolio in case the interviewer wants to share them with another person right then to do an instant interview with you.

6. Be prepared to "show and tell" something from your work history. If you were an architect in your home country, share your portfolio. If you engineered a systems solution, bring the design to show and discuss. If you created a marketing plan, newsletter, or promotional piece, bring it. You can hide the

prior company name if there is a confidentiality aspect. This sharing shows your work itself and you can demonstrate pride. And you will come alive in your facial expression and enthusiasm when you share your work! The interviewer can imagine you doing this kind of work for the employer as well. She can see your passion and your ability to contribute. Practice describing your work.

7. At the end of the interview, if the interview does not mention next steps you can inquire by saying something like "When do you plan to fill this position?" or "What will be your next steps as you interview candidates?" The answer will give you some indication of timing and how interested the company may be in you as the best candidate.

8. Have a strong closing sentence to end the interview. Practice saying it in advance. This should be about why you would be great for the job and that you really want it. If the interviewer says, "Is there anything else?" you can give a sentence you have prepared and practiced. If the interviewer does not, when the interviewer thanks you, it is probably acceptable for you to say something like "I appreciate your time. I just want you to know that my previous work developing a marketing plan for a product like yours will make me a great candidate for this role, and I am most anxious to work for your company."

You want to look highly organized and professional in the U.S. manner. You will stand out as being prepared, and the interviewer will see you talking as if you have worked on their business already. This kind of preparation will overcome any hesitation the interviewer might have as to whether you as a foreign-born candidate will grasp the workplace and be a good fit.

If the company is interested in you at this point, they may ask you for references. Next, we will discuss how to handle this request.

REFERENCES

A company that wants to move forward with you is likely to ask for several references. References are people they can call who will tell the company's hiring manager or HR professional that you are a good person, a good worker and that you will perform well in the job they are considering offering to you. How do you select references and let the references know they may be called to support your job interview process?

Case Study:

PADMA, AN OFFICE MANAGER FROM INDIA

A U.S. executive got an unexpected call from a university employer asking her to be a reference for Padma, a potential employee. Padma was a finalist to work for a university department head. This surprised the woman who was called, as she was not aware of the employer's open position and did not have a good memory of why the international candidate was a good fit for the job. In addition, the woman was not even sure that Padma wanted the job! This could have been easily avoided if Padma had called her friend in advance and informed her of the job and her interest in the position before the call came.

You can see in this example that the best solution would have been for Padma to notify the reference in advance with information about the job and why she had the skills and interest to perform well.

If you are interested in a job and the company asks for your references, this is great news! You want to give them the names of people who know you and know why you will be a good employee. It is an incredibly good sign if the organization reaches out to your references. If you apply for a job and put down a person as a reference, notify that person immediately that you have listed them as a reference. This gives you a chance to tell the reference about the exact job you are applying for and the three reasons you are right for the job. In that way, when the reference is called about you, your reference is ready to be your best supporter.

Why This Works

The company wants to know that you are a good candidate who has supporters. This adds to your value in their assessment of you. You never want to have a potential reference be surprised or say they do not want to be your reference if called. In addition, you do not want the reference person to give support points about you that are not relevant to the job you are hoping to be offered.

You want to give the reference all the information in advance, so they are not surprised to hear from the employer. Please give the reference person the job description, the company information, the résumé you used for that specific job, the cover letter you used, and the top three skills you want the reference to point out in their comments about you. This will allow the reference to respond quickly and with the key work attributes that point to you as the best candidate for the job. And it gives the reference a positive feeling about you as a candidate because you made it easy for them to support your job interest.

RESILIENCE AND RESPONSE

It often takes much longer to move through the interview process than you may expect, even if each step of the interview process has gone well. Also, there may be many steps between the decision of a company to hire you and when you receive the job offer. Here is a situation where the job process took much longer than expected and caused frustration that could have resulted in a potentially damaging behavior.

Case Study:

THUC, A HEALTHCARE WORKER FROM VIETNAM

It was taking a long time to find a job. Thuc was frustrated. There was a long delay in hearing from an employer after applying. A good interview and then, no response. A different employer had treated him rudely in the process, dismissing his skills and in some ways dismissing skills obtained in his home country. Thuc was tempted to write an email back that was true and honest, though it would not be what the hiring recruiter wanted to hear. The candidate was even tempted to write a slightly masked negative story about the employer on his social media account. He was encouraged to vent his feelings to us and to others who were in his personal circle of friends but not online. It was explained to him that a different future employer could be put off by reading negative comments on social media because he had written about others in the job search process.

It is extremely hard to be patient with employers and the job search process. You must show a calm and patient exterior to those who interview you. This is what resilience means. They want to see "the best you." If you need to vent your frustrations, find that trusted friend or someone in the field (who is not in the company you are interviewing) with whom you can share your frustrations. Then, put that happy face and pleasant voice tone back in place for the next interaction with your possible new employer. Even if you get an initial "no," stay positive, because things do change.

There are cases where an original "no" to a candidate after an interview changed to a "yes" within a few weeks. In one case, the company created a new job for the person as the business grew and wanted to talk to interview the candidate further. In another, the first candidate did not work out and they called our international person who had been the second choice to take the job. Remember, the "no" may not be a final answer. Always communicate a good attitude as you look forward, and it will reflect well on you in ways you may not even realize at the time.

Another challenging part of the interview process can be discussing visas and work authorization.

VISA AND WORK AUTHORIZATION DISCUSSIONS

Some of the most difficult issues involve questions about visas or work authorization if you are not already authorized. You need legal input for these questions and should consider these cases and discussion points as possibilities to consider in advance of your job process, not legal advice.

Case Studies:

AIKA, A MANAGER FROM JAPAN

Aika was networking and meeting many potential employers at career fairs and events. She was encouraged to apply by those she met who liked her skills and interactions. However, she did not yet have her employment authorization in hand. She expected to have it in the coming months.

PIERRE, AN INTERNATIONAL STUDENT FROM FRANCE

Pierre was graduating soon with a STEM (science, technology, engineering, and math) degree. He was applying to jobs and wanted to know how to answer the question on the online application: "Will you need visa sponsorship?" He believed that if he answered "yes" his application would not move forward. And, because he could work for three years with his optional practical training (OPT and OPT-STEM) he did not technically need visas sponsorship yet, although he would down the road if the company wanted to retain him.

CUONG, A MARKETING STUDENT FROM VIETNAM

Cuong was an international student who had a marketing degree (non-STEM). He was doing his one year of optional practical training (OPT) work in a company and expected that he would return to Vietnam at the end of the year when his visa expired. He met an American citizen and got engaged, so his fiancée visa followed by marriage allowed him to stay. He ultimately became an American citizen.

CHARLES, A BUSINESS EXECUTIVE FROM ENGLAND

Charles, a senior executive international business leader, was on an H1B visa (a typical work visa for an international corporate hire) for a three-year work term with his employer. He wanted to understand how he could change employers and what steps the new employer would need to understand right from the beginning of his conversations with them.

Each of these examples is unique, and your situation will be as well. You are likely to need the advice of an immigration attorney for work-related needs. For international students, your international student office and career service offices will advise you. Advice given here is just for example; you will need your own legal advisor because situations change based on U.S. law at the time, your home country, your work, your education level, your company's work locations and many other factors that only you and your immigration attorney can manage. You will find a path forward with legal advice.

If you have a short-term visa but not a longer-term visa, hold off discussing work authorization and the longer-term visa sponsorship needs, if possible, until the later interview stages. Work to build a good personal rapport and showcase what your skills would add to the company. Often, you may have student projects which can demonstrate your talents to a company. Try to make the personal connections as strong as possible before you need to discuss hiring considerations. If you are seen as adding great value, the company may work to find a specific role or work relationship that will allow you to continue with the company in the U.S. or even outside the United States.

If you will need visa sponsorship to stay and work for the company, you need to answer truthfully on the application. In today's more mobile world, the company may be able to consider you for a U.S.-based job or may be interested in having you work for the company from your home country. While this may not meet your goal of staying in the U.S. longer, it can buy you time for other actions to happen in U.S. immigration law or in your personal life that might change your immigration status.

Why This Works

If a company sees that you will add value and contribute to the goals of the organization, the company leaders will want to find a way for the lawyers to have you work for them. It is up to you to show more than what a résumé can show. When you demonstrate energy, persuasion, technical skills, and great interpersonal connections, working relationships will happen through the visa process. Show your greatness early in the discussion process!

If you are not getting interviews or job offers, you may want to add some additional work experience to your skill sets and résumé. If you keep improving your skills, you will ultimately be successful in your job search. The next section describes ways you can do that.

ADDITIONAL WORK EXPERIENCE: PROJECTS, INTERNSHIPS, MENTORSHIPS, AND JOB SHADOWING

Getting a job offer for a U.S. job is a big deal. If you are not having success in your job search yet, you may need some additional skill-enhancement opportunities. There are some less-obvious and more-flexible ways to add experience and work connections to your résumé. Here are some ways to add that extra work knowledge to your skill sets. You will see examples of projects, internships, mentorships, and job shadowing.

Case Studies:

TEAM OF INTERNATIONAL STUDENTS FROM LOCAL UNIVERSITY: A PROJECT

A team of international students did a final capstone research project for their degree. This was done for the St. Louis Mosaic Project. The students did company interviews in the community, did reviews with their workplace project supervisor, and presented a final report. They got to see how a U.S. organization worked, talked with U.S. employers, and built their confidence for their future job searches.

NOR, AN INTERNATIONAL ENGINEERING STUDENT FROM MALAYSIA: AN INTERNSHIP

Nor worked through her school's designated school official (DSO) and secured a summer internship with an engineering firm under curricular practical training (CPT). This exposed her to the workplace and broadened her network of potential contacts for her future job search.

IZZET, A BUSINESS STUDENT FROM TURKEY: A MENTORSHIP

Izzet was matched with a local business leader through a program of a leading St. Louis business professional organization. He was matched with the head of the World Trade Center St. Louis. Through this arrangement, Izzet benefited from a close local relationship and introductions to many more people in the St. Louis global business community over the course of the year.

SAANVI, A MARKETING MANAGER FROM INDIA: A JOB-SHADOWING EXPERIENCE

Job shadowing is a way for someone to spend a short time, possibly one day or a few half days, watching alongside a working professional. In this case, Saanvi spent a day with a local marketing executive at the headquarters of a retail chain. Saanvi was able to hear the way the U.S. marketing team talked about products, pricing, promotion, and placement. She heard about the company's e-commerce growth. And she got a sense of the way the U.S. workplace operated. This experience helped her interview more successfully in the future for a job at a different organization.

In each of the cases above, the international job seeker got new information and new contacts. It all adds up to an improved chance of getting a job faster.

Find a way to get exposure to the U.S. workplace and the people who work here. Some job seekers think this must be an official internship, which can be hard to get. Why are internships so hard to get? A company often uses the internship to test a potential future employee relationship. If the company does not sponsor work visas, they may have a rule to not have international people in the internship positions. So you need to find other ways to get this work experience and exposure. Be creative! You can find a way to spend time learning and experiencing an American company if you are thoughtful and persistent.

In summary, if you need to boost your résumé and your network to get a job, look for a way to do a one-day shadow experience, a project in a company for a paper, or a chance to interview an executive. These experiences will add to the people in your LinkedIn network. Keep up communications during the year with the people you meet in these ways by sharing periodic updates about your job search. If you impress them with your skills and engagement, the people in these organizations might find a way to hire you for future work.

Why This Works

For every company that says it does not sponsor a visa, we have seen it happen for some unusual person who is compelling. But an organization will not know how wonderful you are if you do not get in front of them! You need to find any way to get through a company's door and meet its workers to show your interest.

If you are making relationships through your university faculty or your community connections, find a way to suggest a project or a short-term experience that gets you in the door. A short job-shadowing experience does not usually take corporate approval from the HR department. The experience can be a day or a week during a January term or a summer break. You must be resourceful and maneuver yourself to make those personal connections that pay off in future work opportunities. You can do it!

Through the interview process and any discussions of work authorization or references, you need to thank many people. Here is more information on how to do that well.

THANK-YOU LETTERS TO EMPLOYERS AND THOSE WHO GAVE ASSISTANCE

If you had an interview or meeting with a possible employer or helpful person, you should write a thank-you letter via email or a notecard. The same goes if a person has been helpful to you in the search process overall. Thanking someone for their job search assistance keeps you in their mind and makes it more likely they will help you again.

Case Studies:

SAOIRSE, A DATA ANALYTICS MANAGER FROM IRELAND

Saoirse finished her interview, and the next day she sent a positive and appreciative email to the hiring manager. This note thanked him for the interview and stressed the three reasons she was so interested in working with him at the company. Another person who had interviewed did not write a thank-you email. Guess which person got the job? Correct: Saoirse, who wrote the positive and personal thank-you email stating how much she wanted the position. Was it because of the thank-you note? No, but it put her ahead of the other candidate and made the employer think the best of her ability to contribute going forward.

CHINAKA, A MANUFACTURING MANAGER FROM NIGERIA

Chinaka received several introductions to people in different companies by one specific person he met at an industry event. He never let that person know what happened after these introductions or how his search was going. A few months later, the helpful friend saw on LinkedIn that Chinaka had started working at one of the companies where he had made an introduction. The helpful friend felt surprised that Chinaka had not been let him know or thanked him for the assistance. The friend contacted Chinaka to congratulate him, and then Chinaka was very appreciative of the help. He apologized for getting so busy he forgot to let the friend know of his success.

You can see in the first case that being appreciative was a positive factor in getting a job. In the second case, the lack of appreciation hurt the worker's chance to get help from the originally helpful friend in the future. When you thank a potential employer or a person who helps you, it makes the recipient feel positive toward you. It makes them more motivated to help you in the future and to help you with career advancement advice as you progress.

One week, the team at the St. Louis Mosaic Project got calls from two people who had finally landed new jobs. We had assisted them in networking and making professional connections. For one, we had made personal calls and sent notes to key people in the hiring process for the specific job. For the other, we had been a friendly and supportive part of his search. It was so rewarding to hear that each had found a good position with the right responsibilities and pay. And there may be future ways we can assist in career development and career connections for them in the future. Both people with new jobs told us they look forward to helping us help others once they get settled — they understand now that having strong work connections helps all of us make the region a better place to work and live.

Sometimes we get a handwritten note from someone we helped. This really stands out, and we share it within our work team. We feel honored that the person made the time to thank us and others who helped on the job path. A handwritten note or email should also be written to a hiring manager during the interview process, but emails seem to be the fastest method currently used to thank those you meet during the interview process itself.

Making the time to thank others shows appreciation and makes the recipient think more highly of your interpersonal skills.

Why This Works

Taking the time to write the email or handwritten note makes you stand out. It shows your humanity, and it shows your interest in both the work and the person you met. Most candidates do not do this, so you can shine as an outstanding candidate.

SUMMARY OF STAGE III

Interview Process and Preparation

1. Understand the differences between the kinds of interviews you may experience.
2. Learn about the chronological and behavioral interview methods.
3. Determine which of your skills match the skills most desired by U.S. employers.
4. Prepare and practice your interview skills with a trusted person.
5. List the people who could be a reference for you.

6. Understand how to talk about your work authorization.

7. If you are not getting interviews and job offers, consider getting more experience to add to your résumé and network of potential employers.

8. Send thank-you emails and notes to those who interview you and those who help you.

Now that you have managed your interview process, how will it work when that desired job offer comes your way? It will happen, and the next section, on accepting a job offer, will recommend how to make this important decision work for your personal, career and financial goals.

USE THIS SPACE TO TAKE NOTES *about how to do a great job in your interviews through preparation of your interview skills. You may want to review examples of chronological and behavioral interviews. You may want to list companies that are tops on your list of potential employers so you can research people and online information about their interview processes.*

STAGE IV

Accepting a Job Offer

After all your hard work, it appears you are going to be getting that exciting job offer! Let's discuss how to handle this wonderful next step in your life.

Case Studies:

HYUN, A FINANCIAL MANAGER FROM KOREA

Hyun was excited to be offered a good job by a financial services company. She called her mentor to ask if she should accept the offer. Together, they reviewed all the components of the offer: the salary, the benefits including insurance and paid time off (PTO) for sick days, holidays, and vacation. The salary was extremely low compared to similar jobs she saw on www.salary.com and other job salary websites as well as low in terms of what she was expecting. Still, this job was with a good company and was a return to her finance industry experience after her move to the U.S.

Another concern was that the days off listed in the job offer were extremely limited and would make it difficult for her to visit her family in Korea in the next year. We suggested she get back to the company with a strongly positive response about wanting to accept the job and ask if they would consider raising the salary by a certain amount to be more in line with what she was expecting to receive as well as ask that they grant her five more paid days off annually. She also re-stated that she was looking forward to starting work for them in the coming weeks. After waiting a few nervous days, their HR person wrote back that they could raise the salary a small amount but not the dollar increase requested, and they could add three additional paid days off and two unpaid days annually. Hyun immediately wrote back that she was excited to accept the offer and to begin working.

GAMAN, AN IT MANAGER FROM INDIA

Gaman had been searching for a technical position for almost a year. He had been in second and third rounds of interviews but ultimately was not the final candidate. He was depressed and frustrated. Finally, two companies expressed interest, and he made it to the final rounds. One company made him a job offer but the salary was lower than expected. The benefits were good. He discussed with an advisor friend whether he should accept the offer as is or ask for more salary before accepting. He decided that because he really wanted to accept the job and start working, he would not ask for more dollars in salary but would ask if it would be possible to have a six-month salary review instead of a one-year review and if he could have three extra paid vacation days annually. The company came back agreeing to an earlier-than-usual salary review date and the three additional vacation days annually. Gaman started the job and was relieved to be back in the work force.

These cases show that you may have an ability to ask for a little bit more than what an original offer provides if you do so in a polite and positive way that shows you plan to accept the position with excitement. This does not mean you must accept the job but puts you in a good light to get a few more benefits in the job-offer stage. Let's look at some good ways to communicate and negotiate a better salary and benefits package after you receive your offer in writing (either via email or on paper).

JOB OFFERS AND NEGOTIATIONS

In the U.S. it is typical for an employer to not put everything possible into the original job offer, meaning the salary plus benefits package. The HR professional or the hiring manager will not be surprised if you ask for a slightly better offer for one or two elements of the offer. You must do this in a pleasant and positive way and not in a way that implies you will turn down the job if your request is not possible. If the offer is already attractive to you in terms of salary and other components, then accept it as is right from the start, as there is nothing wrong with accepting the offer as given to you.

But if you feel that the job merits a slightly higher starting salary and better benefits in terms of any health benefits or savings benefits plus PTO, then you should inquire. You can write "I am interested in working for your company. Is it possible to consider X and Y?" Another option is to ask if you can be given several days of unpaid time off to add to paid vacation days if you need more time to travel out of the country to visit family far away.

You need to prepare yourself for this conversation. It is an awkward part of the discussion when you suggest a new increased offer for the employer to consider. Be ready for this part of the U.S. job process. If never feels comfortable. Research the nature of the offer and then practice the discussion with a family member or trusted friend. This will make your request feel more natural when this actual part of the conversation happens.

Why This Works

If the job market is strong for you as an applicant and the employer wants you to accept the offer, they will be looking to agree to one or two things that you suggest would make their job offer better for you. The company's representative in HR may have the authority to grant one or two of these requests. If they made the offer, it means they want you and will try to accommodate your additional requests to a small extent. If there is no flexibility and they tell you they cannot change the standard offer that everyone in that role receives, then you need to decide if you will accept. If so, you should respond in a positive way that you appreciate the company representative checking on your behalf and look forward to accepting the offer as is.

If you are successful in your work experiences and interviewing, you may find that the employer will need an immigration lawyer to hire you and do the paperwork. The process is not expensive for the company in comparison to your salary and the benefits you bring to them. You can suggest a good immigration lawyer to a company, as you will see in the next chapter.

USING IMMIGRATION LAWYERS

Some examples below give ideas of the ways you can use immigration lawyers to get and maintain your legal work status in the U.S. The examples show the range of ways that immigration lawyers can help with your U.S. workplace goals; these examples do not represent legal advice.

Case Studies:

MEIHUI, AN INTERNATIONAL BUSINESS STUDENT FROM CHINA

Meihui called because a company wanted to hire her but did not know how to go about the process. The good news was that she was so compelling in her skills that the hiring manager was extremely impressed. The challenge was to quickly get the company to consult with several immigration lawyers to see which one would be a good fit to determine how to make this hiring action happen and what the series of steps would be. The student checked with her school and other resources to quickly give the company the names of three immigration lawyers.

ADESH, A GRADUATE STUDENT IN BIOSCIENCES FROM INDIA

Adesh had exceedingly unique skills and globally recognized, peer-reviewed papers. He wanted to understand if a lawyer could help him get a visa based on his skills, not based on an employer. The O and E visas have some opportunities in this way. He consulted with several lawyers and then hired one to pursue a visa based on his exceptional level of scientific abilities and proven success.

AGATHE, A FINANCE STUDENT FROM LUXEMBOURG

A mid-size financial company that did not have an immigration attorney on staff needed recommendations for an immigration lawyer because they wanted to hire Agathe, an international student graduating with a degree in finance. They were drafting a new job description and wanted advice on how to create and post this specific job in a way that would appeal to international clients.

ANDRES, AN INTERNATIONAL IT MANAGER FROM FRANCE

A growing tech company met Andres at a tech conference. He was visiting the U.S. from France. The company found an immigration lawyer to review the ways in which Andres could work for the company.

Did you see a situation like yours in this list? Or of someone you know? Let's look at advice on the topic to see how legal situations can be successfully managed.

There are as many immigration issues as there are international people who want to work and/or live in the U.S.! Every foreign-born person you meet has an immigration and visa story about their pathway to living and working in the United States. Your case is unique, and you are likely to need an immigration attorney at some point to help you successfully navigate the work process.

The world of immigration law keeps changing. This will continue with different U.S. presidents and Congress. Overall, when U.S. unemployment numbers are low and there are unfilled jobs in the technology, agriculture, service, and healthcare industries, there will be a push by the business community to expand legal working visas.

Why This Works

The immigration process is a balance between U.S. policies, a hiring organization, and the candidate. It has specific steps and a pace all its own, regardless of your desire to begin work and the organization's need to get your skills in place. Be aware that you must add extra value to make these extra costs and steps worthwhile to the company hiring you. And of course, if you are already a lawful permanent resident, a U.S. Citizen, or have a visa that allows you to work without sponsorship, put that fact below your name and contact info on your résumé to make the hiring company see that you can start immediately without the costs or expertise needed, as described in this segment.

We can learn more from Nalini Mahadevan, an immigration lawyer who works with individuals, companies, and non-profit entrepreneur organizations to determine how to have the right legal immigration issues resolved. An immigrant herself, she has passion to help others.

EXPERT CONTRIBUTOR

*Nalini Mahadevan,
Immigration Attorney*

Why do you need an immigration attorney? What is the best way to get through the application process with U.S. Citizenship and Immigration Services (USCIS)?

The U.S. has a complex and nuanced immigration ecosystem of statutes, regulations, memorandums, frequently asked questions (FAQs), and guidance issued by U.S. Department of Labor, Department of State, Department of Homeland Security, and other federal agencies, as well as 50 state-enacted criminal and civil laws. In addition, case law from both the federal and state justice systems interprets state and federal statutes and regulations. U.S. immigration law can issue over 185 types of visas for temporary visits, doing business in the U.S.A. to work here, for family, for refuge, and for employment. Visas can allow temporary or permanent stay. Some visas come with tax implications for the applicant; others require prior authorization or registration with the federal government before applying. Above all, this complex system is updated daily with new laws and regulations.

The H1B visa is the workhorse of employment visas in the U.S. The demand for these visas far exceeds the supply, which is limited to 65,000 visa a year (cap-based, i.e., limited availability). There are an additional 20,000 for those with master's degrees earned in the U.S. The application for the H1B visa is time controlled, and the process has changed over the past few years, with a major change in 2020. The H1B visa gives the applicant the ability to work with a future path to living permanently in the U.S. As H1B numbers are limited, there is a demand for work-arounds outside the cap. For instance, there are work visas that are reserved for citizens of Australia, Chile, Singapore, Mexico, and Canada based on treaties between the U.S. and these countries. Some U.S. employers, such as non-profit universities and hospitals, may apply for H1B visas outside the cap anytime during the year. Other work visas, like L visas, are suitable for intracompany transferees and have no limit.

Our law firm has represented a rural hospital to recruit lab technicians from overseas on H1B visas; a chiropractic college who wanted to employ a chiropractor in a joint program with another private business; and a school district that was hiring foreign language, math, and science teachers. These employers had one thing in common: They had to prove they were exempt from the cap and could apply for an H1B visa any time of the year.

Students at U.S. universities fuel the demand for H1B visas. If they are not chosen in the cap, then the student must find another path to working and living in the U.S. Students can apply for work authorization for either one or three years after completing their degree. The student's undergraduate or graduate degree is the basic determinant of their possible career path, so if academic study is complete, it is almost too late and expensive to change course to qualify for the H1B visa. If you are a student, think about your career path for the next five to 10 years. Is your academic qualification versatile enough to adapt to the changing U.S. economy and enable you to stay on a work visa to legally work in the U.S.? Do your qualifications or degree have an edge over other applicants, especially if you are from India or China? What makes employers beat a path to your door and spend thousands of dollars to employ you?

The plan of action for any person who wants to work and live in the U.S.A. starts in high school before college courses are chosen, because some careers are in demand, and others are not. The challenge is always to match academics with jobs that the employer is willing to sponsor for a work visa.

As for current H1B visa holders, do not be afraid to switch your career path. Make that career jump, go back to school, and sharpen your skills to become 'in demand' — from, say, architect to civil or construction engineering or medical professional. Work in COVID research, move from code writing to data science. Negotiate with your employer about sponsoring your visa for your new, in-demand skills. Use your past work experiences as a tool. If you are ready to make a career change and have the necessary qualifications that are recognized here in the U.S., go ahead and make that change. An experienced immigration attorney could assist to make your job description unique and highly specialized to meet the USCIS criteria based on your education and experience.

An immigration attorney will not only help you navigate the visa system but also provide advice on visa strategies and a path to citizenship. The highest demands for work visas are from China and India. Their nationals wait the longest for a green card to permanently stay and work in the U.S.A., sometimes 15 to 35 years. Any mistake that is made in the visa process could result in a denial months or years after the original application is made. Applicants are incredibly stressed by the wait and the complexity of the visa process. Applicants can reduce their wait if their spouse was born in a different country (e.g., not from India or China).

As an immigration attorney who has been practicing in this field for over 18 years, I have had the pleasure of working with clients from different countries with unique challenges and issues. Disclose your "dirty laundry" (bad happenings in your background) to your attorney, such as criminal acts, no matter how small (like cautions in the UK); divorces; parking and traffic tickets; previous, annulled marriages; past USCIS applications; and visa refusals or denials. If you have been involved in a profession that was legal in your home country but illegal in U.S. disclose it to your immigration attorney. For example, habitual recreational marijuana usage or working as an escort/prostitute may be legal in some foreign countries but are not in the U.S. Every aspect of your life is taken into consideration when dealing with USCIS, so it is best to be honest.

In my years of practice, I have seen many cases that were tricky and interesting. Gone are the days when an application to USCIS was easy and simple. I immigrated to the United States more than 30 years ago. I would no longer apply for a U.S. visa without the assistance of an immigration professional.

"

SUMMARY OF STAGE IV
Accepting a Job Offer

1. Understand what salary and benefits are likely for your role and what special needs you may need to request when you respond to a job offer.

2. Get several recommendations for immigration lawyers so you are ready to suggest one if an employer needs assistance to hire you or if you need modifications to your work authorization.

At this point, you've reviewed the material in this book and have gained knowledge on the interview process for jobs in the U.S. You may have even received a job offer! Armed with this information, you may choose to work with an immigration attorney and your hiring organization to ensure all legal issues are taken care of.

What will keep you progressing in your career with your new American colleagues and supervisor? How will you excel in this new work environment? The next section will discuss steps to set you up for your career success in the American workplace.

USE THIS SPACE TO TAKE NOTES *about how to respond to a job offer. You may want to review examples of salary and benefits for your industry, immigration situations like yours, or names of potential immigration attorneys who could assist when an employer wants to hire you.*

STAGE V

Advancing Your Workplace Career

Your job is going well. You are meeting all your work goals. Your supervisor and team feel supportive. But then you wait for advancement that feels slow to come. What can you do to increase your chances for more responsibility, pay, and promotion? You know you are worth it!

QUALITY INTERACTIONS WITH COLLEAGUES

You go to work and do your assignments. You get good reviews for your work itself. But somehow you feel that there are things you are missing in the conversations that are happening among your colleagues. You are accepted by them, but you are not really part of the group that spends quality time together outside of the expected work. You want to break out of that limitation. These cases demonstrate how to do that.

Case Studies:

SANGITA, AN ARCHITECT FROM INDIA

Sangita works for a growing architecture firm. She had been an intern for the company and was hired by them full time upon graduation. In speaking with her in her first few months as a regular associate, she was trying to figure out how to build good relationships and build trust with her colleagues. While the project work was fine, she needed new ways to enhance her interpersonal skills. She did not want to come on too strong, nor did she want to be left out or hang back from getting to know her colleagues the right way. This need to socialize with work colleagues was uncomfortable for Sangita. In her mind, her high-quality work output should be enough. When a work group organized an easy outdoor hiking event, she almost did not attend. Upon reflection, she did attend and was glad she did. She got a ride to the event with a co-worker. She enjoyed getting to know that colleague. At the event, she got to know a few others in a different way than in the work setting. When she talked about the hike the week after the event, she felt good that she had been present and connected in new ways with her colleagues.

JOSÉ, A SCIENTIST FROM GUATEMALA

José was doing excellent work. Yet he wondered why he was not getting considered for promotions. After discussions with mentors, he realized he needed to build stronger personal relationships and trust with peers and those above in the reporting structure in order to advance in his career. He discussed possible ways to do this and began to take steps to form more authentic relationships beyond discussing the work itself. Over time, he was included in more discussions about broader company opportunities, and he put himself forward for additional responsibility and roles. His career advanced.

In both cases above, the interpersonal relationships began to take on more importance. How can you build closer professional relationships with colleagues and supervisors in a comfortable way? Here are ideas you will find easy to use.

It takes work to build multicultural relationships because they often do not happen on their own. When it comes time for lunch or a casual gathering after work, people who are more similar gravitate to each other. So you, the foreign-born person, need to show that you are, in fact, like your native-born colleagues. You must find areas of common interest and structure times to connect on these terms. It could be asking for advice, saying "I would love your opinion on this issue" and suggesting a coffee break or lunch discussion, or sharing an article about a topic with someone you know will find it interesting, then stopping by to discuss it.

Good topics to ask about are children, pets, travel, sports, and restaurants. There is research that says in the U.S. it can be especially important to career promotions that a worker is "likeable," beyond the aspects of whether the person is doing a good (or even excellent) job. Many international professionals find that excelling at their work and not building relationships can give a "likeability gap." And, without that "likeability" factor, great work can result in appreciation for the work but nothing more in terms of promotion or other advancement. In that case, the supervisor supports the person to keep doing the job he or she is already doing. To advance in many workplaces, relationships and trust need to be built at a higher level beyond excelling at the job itself.

It is always a safe question to ask someone about upcoming travel and vacation plans. Where will the person be going over a holiday? Are they planning to drive or fly? What is the route? Have they been before and would recommend it? If you see an article or upcoming event that relates to the destination, send the person the link or drop off information about the event. Follow up to ask for the highlights.

Sports are particularly important in America, especially supporting the "home team" that is based in your city. Learn about the more important local teams: the names of key players, the top rivalries, the opening and closing days of the season. Check on the scores. Then ask colleagues if they follow a local team and use that as your common topic to enjoy sharing. Give it enthusiasm even if you never attend a game!

If there is a sport that many in your office play, especially if they play together, consider learning it. Maybe you will take golf lessons! You will have fun discussing that with your colleagues.

Lastly, restaurants and cooking are great ways to generate discussions and form bonds. Asking what kinds of foods or new restaurants someone likes gives you great information in terms of suggesting new ideas or a lunchtime visit to a new place. You might even share a kolache pastry, Japanese candy, or a new restaurant menu if appropriate.

Why This Works

These ideas create a personal bond in addition to a professional relationship. They are comfortable to discuss with colleagues or those above you in the organization. They do not violate any personal boundaries. These topics show you to be a multidimensional person. And if you drop off some garam masala spice to a colleague who says he likes Indian food or send over a story about the new golf ball material technology to that golfer colleague, it will build a relationship. This kind of activity creates laughter, connections, and good feelings on all sides. Does this take effort and planning? Yes. Is it worth building authentic relationships that will help your work and possible career advancement? Most certainly!

As you develop business relationships, you will hear about the role of sponsors and mentors in helping career advancement. Who are these people and where do you find them? Let's explore that in the next section.

SPONSORS AND MENTORS

American career advice often focuses on the benefits of having sponsors (sometimes called champions) and mentors. This section will explain more about who these people are and the role they can play in your career success.

Case Studies:

JUAN, A MARKETING MANAGER FROM SPAIN

Juan knew he wanted his career to grow and that might mean domestic or international assignments. When he came to the U.S. for his first role, an older executive in Europe thought this would develop his skills. Every year, the European leader spoke with Juan while he was in the U.S. Ultimately, the senior European leader advised Juan to return to Europe, and the senior leader helped arrange this move. The senior leader was his "sponsor," or career guide and could also help make the career moves happen.

KANDA, A BANKING MANAGER FROM THAILAND

Kanda, a rising leader in a company, would call her "mentor" (who was outside the company) every few months to discuss her career. They had a friendship and a positive relationship. They talked about what was going well and what was not so positive in the work arrangement. They talked about differences between the Asian division she had worked in previously versus the American division she worked in now. The mentor shared her experiences and offered ideas and suggestions.

Both recognized that while the mentor did not know the company inside or the internal people, she could still be a support to Kanda. The mentor gave advice and support but was not able to directly make any career moves happen for Kanda.

You can tell from these examples that a sponsor is able to advise you and impact your career from within the company, while a mentor can guide you without having direct impact on your career opportunities. A mentor can be inside or outside your organization.

Moving up in an organization takes time. Much of your advancement will happen based on the positive results you achieve in the work you are assigned to accomplish. There are also intangible aspects of rising in an organization that are hard for an employee to understand, especially an employee who comes from another country and culture. For these reasons, it is a good idea to seek out at least one mentor and one sponsor as you advance in your career. These can change over the years as your level of accomplishment rises, but you always need inside and outside advisors to your career.

To be more specific, a sponsor is someone inside the organization who knows you and your work. They are senior to you and have more expertise in navigating the specific culture of your organization. They have relationships at a higher level than you do and can see some of the benefits of different career paths or skills to gain within the company, as well as push for your next opportunities. You are more likely to get a sponsor after several years at the company, when you have started to build your reputation as someone who does great work and wants to advance in responsibility and level.

Some companies have official programs to assign a sponsor, but usually it is a more personal and professional request that you make of someone high in your company. You need to have already formed some relationship with that person through meetings, presentations, or shared experiences within the company. You then request that the person be a "sponsor" to you by meeting with you a few times a year and helping support your career advancement.

A mentor can be inside your organization or outside. This is a person who can be a guide or coach to you on your career path but does not have any power to make your job change or advance. You set up time periodically with your mentor, possibly quarterly, and come to each session with a few prepared questions to discuss. These questions may be about your work, your relationships with those above you or with peers, or thoughts on training you seek. You use this mentor as a sounding board, a person who cares for you and your success but is removed from your actual work team and reporting relationships. This means that the mentor may stay as your mentor if you change companies. He or she may also advise you on outside opportunities to advance your skills and relationships, such as joining community boards or building more outside professional relationships in your industry.

Why This Works

The American system is one of hard work and personal relationships that advance your career. It takes more than doing a good job in your current position to be promoted or to get additional opportunities. This information often does not come from your direct supervisor or from the HR department, although it can happen that way. There may be other official or informal networks in which you can be a member if you want more focused advice tailored just for your career.

You may also get some information from employee resource groups or business resource groups if those operate in your company. Next, let's see how employee resource groups (ERGs) and business resource groups (BRGs) can have a positive impact on your career.

SUPPORT NETWORKS IN A COMPANY

Companies are increasingly offering support networks or affinity groups within their organizations, often called business resource groups (BRGs) or employee resource groups (ERGs). Here are ways you can use these to your career advantage.

Let's look at two cases where internal support networks helped careers advance.

Case Studies:

EUNJOO, A SUPPLY CHAIN MANAGER FROM KOREA

Eunjoo was working for a large regional company. She had not joined any of the organization's affinity groups, often called ERGs or BRGs. There was one for women, another for all Asians, and one for a diversity council. She was busy with work and her family and did not believe it was worth her time. A friend convinced her to join the Asian group. She did, and eventually became an officer of the group. She organized programming within the company for leadership skills of the group members and connected them to an outside Asian community group. Her leadership skills got noticed at work by those outside the Asian group, including her supervisor. She was asked to take on other broader leadership roles in the general company. One opportunity was to move up in her work area. Another opportunity was to step into a leadership role in the company's corporate United Way campaign. She realized that there were direct and indirect benefits from joining the affinity group for those of Asian heritage within the company.

PABLO, A MANUFACTURING MANAGER FROM ARGENTINA

Pablo worked in a mid-size company that had few others with Hispanic backgrounds. He heard about the Hispanic Chamber of Commerce and joined. It was wonderful to meet many people in the community from a range of Latin/Latin-American countries. And they all worked at other companies in town, places he might consider working in the future. He attended an occasional social event, the annual golf tournament, and a holiday gala. As his company needed to hire more diverse workers, he encouraged the company to join the Hispanic Chamber and to post jobs there to get more diverse applicants. Over time, he built good relationships with Hispanic peers and leaders within his company and from companies across the region.

The first case shows that it can be smart for your career to join a company resource network. It builds your knowledge of other functions in the organization, which may help if you consider new open positions within the organization for career growth. You have someone internal to go to for insight and advice. You may meet new friends in different departments who can help you do your current job better or maybe open doors to new roles. It is a way to show your leadership skills within a group where you may feel more comfortable to step up. It may be easier to show that you have strategic, analytical, or creative skills in your work for the ERG than in your regular job. And, if the company supports the ERG by allowing you to spend work time on it, that can mean the company values it. Some companies give the groups a small budget to encourage their success in planning receptions, speakers, or mentoring programs.

In the second case, having an outside network is valuable in the short term and the longer term. Not only does it help compare your own organization and job to others, but it opens your eyes to what the region truly offers for work opportunities. It gives you a way to make authentic relationships outside your work team and your family networks. And you can gain leadership skills and higher recognition for your abilities that can reflect well on your work promotion possibilities.

Why This Works

Companies usually value and promote individuals who are already demonstrating higher-level skills. If one candidate has potential and another candidate shows potential and proves she is doing higher-level strategic planning, analytic, and/or creative skills for an affinity group, the proven candidate will get the higher job promotion.

Another reason these groups are valuable is that companies and jobs are not always stable. Your division could be downsized, the company bought, and your function no longer needed. You lower your career risk if you make the friendships and relationships in affinity groups and community organizations in advance of needing the connections. Then, if you do need help in terms of references, job leads, or insights into new opportunities, you will have created the way for your future job stability.

HIGHLIGHT YOUR PERFORMANCE AND CONTRIBUTIONS TO GET PROMOTIONS AND PAY INCREASES

Many international people come from backgrounds where being humble is a benefit and shining a light on your own performance is not viewed in a positive way. This section talks about why the American organizations view this differently and how you can incorporate this knowledge for your career advancement.

Case Studies:

AMAN FROM AFGHANISTAN

Aman was doing well at this job. He got good reviews. He got the average pay increase in years when the company had raises. He got along with his boss and colleagues. But he never was asked to interview for higher jobs, never promoted, and never asked to lead a new project. He noticed that the people who put themselves forward, asked for new opportunities, brought new ideas to company leadership, and built personal relations were the ones who got bigger opportunities with more pay and financial benefits.

SEO-JUN, AN ANALYST FROM KOREA

Seo-Jun was doing a great job at her company. She was also volunteering for an organization for young professionals in the arts. In fact, she just received their Volunteer of the Year award. She did not mention it at her workplace because she did not want to be perceived as boastful or egotistical.

The first case showed a worker who accepted his role but did not ask for more. In the second case, there was a worker who was modest in a way that limited how her company saw her potential. The U.S. workplace favors employees who seem interested in taking on new, higher levels of opportunity. This means that you must ask for the opportunities. They will not come to you just because you are doing an excellent job at your current work responsibilities. Women born in the U.S. and foreign-born men and women tend to think that if they do a good job, they will get advanced. They learn the hard way that this is only one part of what's necessary.

You need to practice asking for more opportunities and prepare yourself for not getting what you ask for half of the time. But it will be noted that you asked, so when the next opportunity arises, you may be considered.

It is important that you ask in a way that is respectful and not like you are entitled or expect the new assignment or promotion. You need to find a way to say, "I think I will be the best person to take on the new area for the organization because of these two reasons…" And then say no more. If the answer comes back negative, just take it in stride and realize that if you are not selected now, you may be next time. But if you do not ask, you will probably never be considered, because those higher up think you are perfectly content to stay right where you are.

Asking for a pay increase is a difficult conversation. Sometimes there is an annual review cycle when your work is evaluated and a raise is possibly given. You may not have any input regarding that decision. There is a trend toward more frequent evaluations, but evaluations may or may not be tied to pay changes. It is important that you find out if you are being paid fairly. There are sites like **www.salary.com** and others that can tell you the ranges for your job in your city based on experience and work contributions.

If you want to ask for a salary increase, do your homework. Write down what you have contributed. Find a time to meet with your manager in person, if possible. This is not the right time for an email. It is a personal discussion where you put forward that you believe you are adding more value than what you are being paid, based on outside information and your added contributions. You can ask for a raise and see if that is possible for the company to consider. This must be done in a pleasant and positive way. You want your supervisor to hear you, to understand why you are making this request. Even if the answer you get back is a "no" or "not at this time," your supervisor will know that you believe you are worth more and that can impact future raises in a positive way.

In addition, if you receive an award or recognition in an industry group or other organization outside your workplace, you should find a comfortable way to bring this to the attention of your supervisor or department head. Imagine if Seo-Jun had done this and it had brought her positive attention or a new project opportunity! The same can happen to you. If you would like to tell your manager, a nice way is to put it in an email, such as, "I thought you would like to know that I received recognition as the Volunteer of the Year for the young arts group in which I am a member." Using that wording does not sound boastful or like you are bragging, but that you think the supervisor would like to know. Your supervisor may or may not respond about it, but it will be noticed and will be viewed as making you a more valuable employee because others see you as valuable. Your organization may ask to put a note about this recognition in a company newsletter, and you should agree. You can always attribute your recognition to your work with the larger team toward an important goal you believe in, showing that you are a true team player. But do not hide your recognition or special honors! Find a comfortable way to share the good news at your workplace.

Why This Works

Supervisors and hiring managers want to find ways to say "yes" to a good employee sometimes, and they will be impressed if you ask for more responsibility, propose a pay raise at the right time, or get outside awards or recognition. You need to ask strongly for different things that will allow you to do better work or to bring more skills to the organization. Should you ask to attend a special training course? Should you ask to get a certificate in a new skill? Should you ask to lead a special analysis team for a new opportunity? Should you ask for a certain workspace you prefer if the work environment is being re-configured due to more people working from home? Do you want to work remotely one day per week to focus more on new ideas to build the business? If you ask in a pleasant way and are accepting if the current answer is "no" or "not now," you will find that you get some answers of "yes" in the future and your career and pay will grow. And if you share outside recognition, it will reflect well on your future opportunities for pay increases and promotion within the organization.

As organizations measure who is getting promotions and opportunities, some organizations are linking these metrics to their diversity, equity, and inclusion (DEI) initiatives for talent attraction and retention. The next chapter shows how DEI builds a better team and can open more opportunities for you as a foreign-born employee.

DIVERSITY, EQUITY, AND INCLUSION (DEI) AT WORK

Diversity, equity, and inclusion (DEI) are key metrics for successful companies in the United States. More organizations now track the range of backgrounds and ethnicities of their workforce. They also track the pay and promotions of these groups in relation to other groups within the company.

Some organizations reward executives for hitting improved metrics for these measurements. The desire to be a preferred employer as well as the increasingly multicultural workforce require that organizations evaluate their hiring, promotion, and community commitments to reflect the communities in which they operate. This provides a great opening for more international people to add to diversity within organizations.

Case Studies:

A BANK BEGINNING THE DEI JOURNEY

A bank had just organized itself into different teams to develop learnings and structures for a diversity, equity, and inclusion plan. They were looking to understand the needs of their internal associates, their suppliers, their customers (both business and commercial) and the community at large. They sought ideas on demographics, programs, communities, and trends that were possible to be discussed and leveraged for the bank's benefit.

A UTILITY COMPANY WITH A WELL-DEVELOPED DEI PROGRAM

A large company had a well-developed DEI organization and structure internally. They had employee resource groups, a proactive leadership council that invited diverse speakers from the community to educate the group, and an annual conference they sponsored. This annual conference presented leading ideas about diversity: what it meant, who it involved, the language to use, the way the company would grow in its associate base, and understanding this evolving topic serves the community. While the conference's main participants were company employees, they opened it up to key community partners to share their work and to allow others to learn from the speakers.

A COMMUNITY NON-PROFIT THAT BUILDS DEI CAPACITY IN INDIVIDUALS AND ORGANIZATIONS

The Diversity Awareness Partnership in St. Louis educates about all kinds of diversity: physical, country of origin and status, gender, ability, and more. Every year, it puts on a well-attended conference that is open to the community. There are panels offered and moderated by community members. There are top companies who present and who are sponsors. Diversity leaders from business, academia, and non-profits attend. It is a large and joyful event that gives each participant new ways to consider the range of humanity and how we each fit, as well as how we can support each other to lead productive and fulfilling lives.

Each of the above examples shows a way that foreign-born people fit into the growing diversity, equity, and inclusion movement in the U.S.

Organizations committed to DEI are hiring staff, identifying internal experts, and using consultants to assess where they are, where they want to be, and how to get there. It is usually obvious when the organizations do not have good representation of diverse people versus diversity in the surrounding communities, and the companies are seeking to change this. Many have told their HR teams to find ways to identify a broader applicant pool to cultivate more diverse talent pipelines.

If a company is not mentioning this topic and has no aspirations listed to do better, it might still be a wonderful employer and have great jobs. They may have a culture that already values diversity based on its founder or its community partnerships. So dig a bit deeper. Try to find someone from your community who works there, or look at their LinkedIn people listings to see the kinds of employees who work there.

Sharon Harvey Davis is a highly respected expert in DEI on both a local and national level. You will see in her words how you can contribute to the diversity in an organization.

EXPERT CONTRIBUTOR

Sharon Harvey Davis; Vice President of Diversity, Equity, and Inclusion; Chief Diversity Officer; Ameren

Starting a new job is tough. Starting a new job in a new culture can be overwhelming. However, picking the right company can make fitting in less stressful and your ability to feel connected to the people and organization you work for easier.

One way to do this is to look for companies that value diversity and inclusion. Companies that value diversity search for people with different viewpoints, backgrounds, and perspectives. These companies will work to incorporate different perspectives, ideas, and viewpoints into decision making.

Inclusion is not a leadership practice that comes naturally to every leader. Leaders may rely on their own understanding or soliciting opinions from a few selected employees as the easiest and fastest way to get to a decision and get the work done. This can lead to a homogeneous way of thinking and acting that feels comfortable to those involved and also gets the work done expeditiously.

Inclusive leadership may initially feel uncomfortable and divisive to a leader accustomed to a more homogeneous approach to decision making. Getting a wider range of opinions and thoughts that may differ from a leader's own perspective or require changes in how work gets done may feel uncomfortable and daunting. However, in the long run, having a wider variety of thoughts and viewpoints included before decisions are made can spur innovation, avoid blind spots, increase creativity, and lead to continuous improvement as energy increases for new ideas.

It is important to know how to find organizations that will value the diversity of thoughts and experiences a diverse workforce will bring to the organization and include those perspective in how they do business. There are several ways to identify companies with a diverse workforce and inclusive culture.

First, look for the organizations that support and are involved with international or diverse organizations. Where a company spends its money and resources will tell you a lot about what they value and what is important to them. The companies that value diversity in their communities will also value diversity in their organizations

Second, look at organizations that specialize in diversity research and analytics. Some of these companies also have methodology to rate and publicly report on corporate diversity and inclusion performance. Companies found on listings or rankings by these companies have either provided information or have public information that has been reviewed to determine the diversity of the workforce and corporate commitment to inclusion, equitable programs, and wide-ranging community support. A few examples of these organizations are DiversityInc and Forbes.

Finally, check a company's website. This should reveal insights into their commitment to a diverse workforce and an inclusive culture. Companies that have a commitment to diversity and inclusion will speak to it on their websites. Look for diversity and inclusion programs, training, and commitment statements.

Also search for employee groups with a diversity focus where employees can come together to help address and solve specific diverse focus areas and create social networks related to a diversity subject or theme. These groups are often called affinity groups, business resource groups, or employee resource groups.

The company website should also provide a glimpse of the diversity in the leadership of company. Learning about the board members and executives in a company can give a greater insight into the seriousness of a company's diversity, equity, and inclusion commitment. A diverse leadership team is more likely to champion a diverse workforce, and it demonstrates that a company's commitment to diversity travels to the highest levels of the organization.

Finding a company that values diversity and includes it in how they do business will allow the many unique qualities and attributes a diverse workforce brings to an organization to grow and flourish. A diverse and inclusive culture allows employees to have a sense of belonging, a smoother integration into the corporate culture, and a greater connection to the work and purpose of the organization. It is worth the extra effort to find the right company that will include and value the unique perspectives you will bring to the organization.

99

SUMMARY OF STAGE V
Advancing Your Workplace Career

- Identify several colleagues with whom you would like to build better interpersonal relationships.

- Consider who might be a good internal sponsor for you and who inside or outside your organization might be a positive mentor.

- Research your organization's offerings of support networks such as an ERG or BRG.

- Find a way to share a success or recognition you receive with those inside your organization. Use this to ask for more opportunities, promotion, or pay increases.

- Read about your desired organization's diversity, equity, and inclusion goals and learn who are the internal supporters of this work.

You have now learned key ideas for your work success. The final section offers special knowledge for unique groups of foreign-born people and advanced career skills for those seeking higher-level professional positions.

USE THIS SPACE TO TAKE NOTES *about ways to advance your workplace career. You may want to list colleagues you would like to get to know better, possible sponsors and mentors, or information about your organization's employee support groups and info on how to reach those groups. You may want to list some accomplishments that you might share more broadly with your supervisor and others in the organization.*

STAGE VI

Special Knowledge

INTERNATIONAL STUDENTS

International students represent the best and brightest in the global economy. The United States hosts close to one million international students annually. A majority are in the STEM (science, technology, engineering, and math) fields. These STEM jobs are needed for U.S. growth, and there are not enough native-born candidates for these jobs right now as the country builds a pipeline of students for future STEM needs.

Case Study:

LAKSHMI, A SOCIAL WORK STUDENT FROM INDIA

Lakshmi was looking for a job that would ultimately result in sponsorship to stay longer in the United States, beyond her one-year OPT (optional practical training). She evaluated the kinds of organizations that have international roles for which sponsorship might be possible and other work opportunities where the employer can apply for a visa without going through the annual visa lottery, which is possible through hospitals and certain research organizations. She got an OPT work opportunity that related to her social work training and kept looking for specific roles that would allow her to stay longer. She ultimately returned to India but did have the benefit of one year of U.S. work experience to build her résumé for the future.

An important piece of advice here is this: Be irresistible! For almost every employer that says it will not sponsor a work visa for international students, we hear that the employer did sponsor a visa for a unique international student. That occurred because that student was compelling due to their skills, knowledge, global connections, and/or ability to perform for the company.

What are the ways that you can get work experience while on your F-1 student visa at your university? Let's look at the main options: CPT, OPT, and OPT-STEM, described below with a few tips to consider.

CPT, OPT, AND OPT-STEM: There are several pathways in which an international student can study and work in the United States. CPT (curricular practical training) and OPT (optional practical training) give short-term work authorization through the university for an international student on a basic F-1 student visa. The opportunity for an additional 24 months for OPT-STEM (optional practical training extension for STEM students) is excellent when an employer writes a workplan for work in the STEM field for a STEM graduate. It is important to understand what programs in your university are STEM qualified and which are not, and the implications of that decision. For example, it is possible that an economics major is not STEM but an econometrics major is STEM, or that one school's data analytics degree is STEM qualified and another is not. Please understand this early in your academic career so you can pick the best major for your skills and ultimate work goals.

MAKE RELATIONSHIPS WORK FOR YOU: For international students, the potential employer will spend extra money, time, and legal fees if they want to apply for future visas after your student F-1 visa and the CPT or OPT process. See the visa section on pages 61-65. What is important for you as a student is to build strong relationships during an earlier internship, a special project, or a faculty research project with a company. These may make someone work extra hard to get their company to hire you.

CAREER FAIRS: Many universities have career fairs. At these career fairs, the employers often indicate whether they will or will not interview international students. Pay attention to this and do not waste your time on those who say they will not do so at the fair. If your school does not identify these employers, do your homework at a website like **www.myvisajobs.com** to see if a company has sponsored visas and for what kinds of jobs.

INTERVIEW PREPARATION: If you know the person who will interview you, do an internet search to learn about the person and any skills or interests you may have in common. See if other international graduates of your university work at the company and touch base with them for advice. Use LinkedIn smartly.

COMMUNICATE WITH EMPLOYERS: For your first communications, use the person's formal name, such as Ms. Smith. Then, the employer may say "Call me Mary," and you can do so. Always speak or write with professionalism and formality at first.

BUILD YOUR NETWORK OF LOCAL PEOPLE WHO MAY HAVE INTERNSHIP OR JOB CONNECTIONS: Many universities have programs where a local family hosts an international student for holidays and periodic dinners. A local family you get to know may be your key to a job network, and they may be very committed to working hard to keep you in the U.S. An additional benefit is that your English language skills will improve as you meet with a local family. So, if your school has a host family or local dinner program, take advantage of it. Not only will you enjoy a good dinner with kind people, but it could also help your job and career opportunities as well. This host family relationship might happen through a religious congregation as well.

WHAT TO WEAR FOR VIDEO AND IN-PERSON INTERVIEWS: Be sure to present a professional appearance and not your student appearance. Remember to hide your dorm or apartment clutter by using a blank wall or folding panels behind you for video interviews.

Global Detroit is known for a range of training programs designed to help the large number of international students in the region get connected to jobs. You will find their specific advice and tips extremely useful.

EXPERT CONTRIBUTORS

Guiqiu Wang, Program Manager, and Steve Tobocman, Director, Global Detroit

The United States has been a top destination for the world's best and brightest university and graduate students. U.S. colleges and universities dominate the world's highest ranked institutions. Many international students pursuing college and graduate degrees in the U.S. possess a strong interest in moving to the U.S. to pursue the American dream. Others desire to return to their home countries but are interested in supplementing their U.S. educational experiences and degrees with experience in the U.S. corporate sector. Such work experiences can help open job opportunities in their home country with U.S. companies abroad or local firms. Regardless of the reason, the U.S. labor market has seen significant growth in the number of international student graduates entering the U.S. workforce on an annual basis. In fact, in recent years roughly twice as many international students have been joining the labor force working on their student visas as practical training experience than the number of H1B visa workers joining the labor force.

While U.S. companies are slowly becoming more familiar with hiring international students through the CPT and OPT programs — accessible to international students studying under the F-1 visa program, which accounts for the vast majority of the over one million international students studying in the U.S. — international students continue to report difficulty securing employment after graduation, even among graduate students in high-demand fields like engineering and computer science.

Global Detroit has connected over 4,000 international students with over 100 Michigan employers through its Global Talent Retention Initiative (GTRI) since its launch in 2011. Working with top universities in Michigan (University of Michigan, Michigan State University, Wayne State University, and others), the program traditionally has hosted large international student job fairs twice yearly, as well as other, smaller events and opportunities for students to connect with employers. More recently, GTRI has included a Global Talent Accelerator (GTA) program to enhance the soft skills of graduating international students seeking employment in the U.S. By providing intensive training about U.S. corporate culture, résumé writing, job search and interviewing skills, and networking, GTA has been able to place over 70% of its participants into jobs.

Below are some of the GTA program's suggestions to help you, the international student, find a U.S. job after graduation.

START EARLY

International students are eager to find well-paying jobs right after gradation to gain valuable professional experience in the U.S. corporate market and to help pay off expensive tuition costs. Most F-1 students, even with approved optional practical training (OPT), only have 90 days from the time the OPT is granted to secure a job offer before they are required to leave the country. Thus, you need to start looking for work well before you graduate.

U.S. employers really value American work experiences. Direct work experience with an American company is a direct indication of your cross-cultural communication skills and ability to thrive in the U.S. corporate environment. Therefore, it is imperative that you accumulate as much relevant American industry experience as early as you can. International students on an F-1 visa are required to obtain certain work authorization, known as curricular practical training (CPT) or optional practical training (OPT) to work here. Use of the CPT to find internships while studying or during the summers between academic years can help you build that experience, but you need to make sure you stay within the limits prescribed by U.S. immigration laws when using the CPT for part-time employment such that you don't exhaust the opportunities to pursue an OPT experience. The OPT experience allows for full-time paid work in your field of study for one year after graduation and two additional years (three years total) for international students with STEM majors who work for employers using the federal e-verify system.

It is in your best interest to start looking for work early into your time studying at a U.S. college or university. You should consult your international student advisors, learn all the related immigration rules and regulations fully, and navigate all the different work opportunities, such as co-ops or internships. You should take full advantage of CPT and OPT to make yourself more competitive in the American job market.

PREPARE STRONG APPLICATION MATERIALS

Nowadays, a simple résumé is not enough. Job searches require a whole array of documents, from traditional résumés and cover letters to social media accounts and LinkedIn profiles. You should not rely on preparing one résumé and cover letter and hoping that they will work for every position you apply for. You must consider who will read your documents and select the most appropriate format for the résumé. Applicant tracking systems (ATSs) are also widely used to screen résumés, which will screen out application materials without specific keywords. You should first determine companies and positions that you want to pursue. Then, you should identify the keywords for technical skills in each job description. It can be extremely helpful to leverage LinkedIn to verify names and prepare application materials accordingly.

LEVERAGE NETWORKING

On average, in America, each corporate job offer attracts 250 applicants. Of those candidates, four to six will get called for an interview and only one will get the job. With a personal connection that a job seeker makes within a company, their chance of getting an interview increases from one in 50 to one in three. Due to cultural differences and language barriers, networking remains the biggest challenge for international students. To succeed in job searches, you need to learn basic networking skills and reach out to as many people as possible. Start with professors and other fellow students. Conduct as many informational interviews as you can. Utilize career offices and the alumni networks. Seek out professional societies and organizations, as well as connections within the local ethnic communities, especially in the business community. You should try to say "yes" to as many invitations as you can. You should seek out mentor relationships if you can and ask to be connected to other professionals. Building those connections early into your U.S. educational experience — as early as your first semester of international study — can give you important long-term benefits.

PRACTICE INTERVIEW

Practice makes perfect. Practicing answers to typical behavioral questions can help to reduce stress and anxiety at interviews and help you demonstrate your best skills during the interview. You are encouraged to take notes of the questions you encounter in interviews and to think about how to improve your answers for future interviews. You should pick one to two key projects that you are most proud of and prepare a short two- to five-minute presentation using the "problem-action-result (PAR)" model to highlight your achievements and skills. You should prepare and practice elevator pitches (your story of why you want to work at the company) of different lengths, from 30 second to two minutes, to make a strong first impression at interviews. For highly technical STEM positions, you might practice making that presentation using a whiteboard and a marker or prepare a PowerPoint slideshow to share if technology allows. Often, you can also send your PowerPoint or other materials in an email after the interview or presentation.

REMAIN POSITIVE

Finding a job is a full-time job. During normal times, it takes an average American college graduate three to six months to secure employment after graduation. The challenge can be more difficult for international students. Perseverance is key to keeping yourself focused and motivated during your job search. It is important to accept that "rejection letters" are a part of the process and not reflective of your true abilities or character. You should not take rejection personally. When things get difficult, you are strongly encouraged to reach out for help. The therapists at the counseling and psychological services (CAP) on campus can provide critical support. No one is alone in this process. The darkest hour is often right before the dawn.

International students represent the world's best and brightest minds. In addition to providing invaluable skills to U.S. companies, many international students have stayed in the U.S., becoming lawful permanent residents and citizens while navigating various immigration processes. International students not only have gone on to lead important companies; many have also started their own businesses. In fact, immigrants have launched more than half of all the billion-dollar startup companies in the U.S., and more than half of those tech founders came to the U.S. as international students. Securing that first U.S. job can be hard work, but we hope these tips help pave the way for you to either gain valuable experience in the U.S. corporate sector or to pursue the American dream.

"

REFUGEES

Refugees are a special group of international people who arrive in our country. They come legally through the United Nations and the U.S. State Department. They are work-authorized immediately. Some have high skills and excellent English. Some come from countries with fewer office skills and less English exposure. They all need jobs to support their families after a few months of U.S. government support. Their work ethic and skills are important to the U.S. economy. And refugees bring diverse cultures to add to our multicultural country. We welcome refugees for humanitarian reasons as well as their contributions to the economic strength of our communities.

Case Studies:

HASSAN, A DOCTOR FROM SYRIA

Hassan arrived as a refugee in the community. His English was fair. Through the International Institute of St. Louis, he was counseled to get a job as a medical technician. This improved his overall English and his knowledge of English medial terms. He also applied and was accepted in another city at their medical center to do a residency in his field, essentially repeating what he had done years ago in Syria. Since he was young enough to start over, he moved and is on his way to becoming a licensed doctor in the U.S.

ABDI AND HIS FAMILY FROM SOMALIA

A Somali family of nine arrived as refugees to the community. Their English was limited, and one child had special needs. Their prior work was in farming. The housing they were placed in upon arrival required a bus ride to get to needed language training and school attendance for the parents and children. The U.S. systems for shopping, transport, currency, schooling, and daily living were all new. The parents were very motivated to get a job. Through our International Institute's workplace team that works with employers in hotels, casinos, hospitals, and manufacturing, Abdi quickly got an hourly manufacturing job. That job required that he take two buses to get to and from the workplace.

These two case studies show how some refugees come with high skills while others arrive with fewer skills for the American market. Both groups show high motivation and ability to contribute to our country and to our communities.

While refugees arrive with legal status to work in the United States, the reality is often much more difficult. The refugee may have lived with his family in a United Nations refugee camp for decades. The family may or may not speak English, and it is key that they all start learning it as quickly as possible. The children will need to start school with the challenges of language and academic needs. The original 90 days of assistance a refugee family receives from the U.S. government runs out quickly. There may or may not be extra federal, state, or local assistance available for housing, food, or job training. Yet the need to pay bills is immediate. Plus, the family must repay the United States government for its travel costs to come to the U.S., which may total in the thousands of dollars.

Most major regions and some smaller communities have at least one refugee resettlement agency that helps the newly arrived refugee families. They get the family into temporary housing and help them with the initial groceries and steps to independence in the U.S. There are often resources at the resettlement agency or with community partners for English skills, computer training, job training, and work skills. Some religious groups or ethnic groups work to support their newly arrived community members. This can accelerate relationships and job references.

The best advice is for refugees to use all the services offered to get their work skills advanced. But they and the community need to understand the family health and culture challenges that may be happening at the same time the family is trying to get economic stability through at least one family member finding a job. As they join the workforce, refugees add to the hard-working employee base in organizations. And refugees start businesses at a higher rate than our native-born people, adding much to our community's economic growth.

If you are a refugee seeking a job, a true expert is Chelsea Hand-Sheridan. Her team has assisted over 500 refugees and other immigrants annually to find employment and has advised refugees from many countries on the process.

"

EXPERT CONTRIBUTOR

Chelsea Hand-Sheridan, Director of Workforce Solutions, International Institute of St. Louis

Unlike many other newcomers to the United States, as an individual with refugee status, you had not planned to be permanently resettled in another country. With this in mind, it is no wonder that refugees are among the most diverse groups of immigrants in terms of educational backgrounds, work experiences, and access to opportunities. Refugees have greatly enriched the U.S. economy and culture for decades, and professionals across industries are hugely in-demand. In this section, we will explore how refugees can enter and advance in the U.S. workforce.

Not all refugees arrive with the same goals, expectations, or experience, but every individual goes through the same processes for resettlement in the U.S. Some individuals have been unable to hold formal work experience while living in refugee camps or have never been able to study due to interruptions in education. Yet others have extensive work experience and professional credentials but were forced to leave or suspend their professional careers due to displacement and had to leave without proof of professional credentials or transcripts. No matter what your experience was before you came to the U.S., most refugees have similar goals upon entry — early employment to achieve economic self-sufficiency. Finding a job right away is key to establishing connection to your new home and gain a U.S.-based work history. You may find it helpful to seek supportive employment services from the resettlement agency to assist you with gaining an understanding of the U.S. workforce. Finding a job may not sound like a difficult task at first, but without experience or understanding of the local job market, in addition to sometimes limited access to education, work experience, or English-language training prior to entering the U.S., this is a major hurdle even in the times of the strongest economies. As a foreign-trained refugee professional, finding work quickly generally means quickly finding an entry-level opportunity outside of your field of expertise. This can be a big blow to your confidence and professional morale initially, but early employment is vital to begin to build your U.S. work experience and provide early stability for basic needs. Industries commonly accessed by refugees for early employment include hospitality, manufacturing, and healthcare. It is important to note that changing not only jobs but careers in your lifetime is commonplace in the U.S.

A first job should never be thought of as a last opportunity for professional employment — this is just your first step.

Career growth through experience helps all workers advance in their professional lives, and refugee professionals are no different, though advancement looks different upon entry to the U.S. Despite sometimes years of professional work experience and credentials, it is not common that foreign-trained refugee professionals immediately enter their former fields of work. As you know, this is due to a lack of immediate direction to know how to enter specific fields, lack of knowledge of how to gain recognition of foreign-earned degrees and credentials, and a lack of U.S.-based work experience/understanding workforce culture, especially "soft skills." Soft skills can include professional communication, interviewing and networking techniques, business etiquette, and building relationships.

Despite these hurdles, it is *not* impossible to return to a former career field, and you do not always need to redo your education entirely! Fortunately, in recent years there has been growth in programming designed to help foreign-trained professionals learn the necessary information regarding licensure, credentialing, in-demand positions, degree equivalency, and evaluation information. Refugee social service agencies and resettlement agencies have developed career-advancement-supportive services geared toward supporting refugees and foreign-trained immigrants re-entering their fields of expertise. Resources such as WES Global Talent Bridge, Upwardly Global, the Welcome Back Initiative, and other programs can provide broad support on how to re-enter career fields nationally. There may be local career pathways programs in your area geared toward refugee and immigrant professionals support.

The process to re-entry may be longer than expected and can seem daunting, but it is important to realize your experience and education are important here in the U.S. Refugees are commonly unable to access original educational and professional documentation such as degree transcripts or licensure information due to the state of their home country/university. If you can access these documents, credential evaluation companies can assist you with recognizing if your degree is equal or similar to a degree from the U.S. Evaluations can convince an employer, university, or state licensing board that you are equally qualified to work in that field as someone with a similar U.S. degree. Sometimes evaluations can show that there are partial credits that need to be completed, but this takes much less time and money than redoing a degree. Other programs, like WES Gateway Program evaluations, can provide some recognition of a degree, though not as a full evaluation. It is important to speak with the employer, state licensing board, or university seeking the degree evaluation before paying for an evaluation to learn which sources they accept. (For more information, check out local board information by profession or generally at **www.NACES.org**.) If you cannot access the original documents to be formally evaluated, fear not. This does not mean that you will be unable work in your professional field in the U.S.

If return to a specific position is not possible due to an inability to gain licensure or access transcripts, this does not mean the end of the road for that career. Look at your technical skills and expertise and review related roles where you can leverage your skills into a different opportunity. This will require an understanding of what may be available locally, but also how you can promote your skills in a related position. Humble yourself to accept a lower position in your field but show your confidence that you can do the job and further enhance your experience. This can be the first step in "getting into" a company. Companies often promote dedicated workers, and getting any access is crucial to further professional development long-term. Another option may be to obtain a short-term skills certificate in your field or to enter an apprenticeship to further highlight your aptitudes, increase your technical skills, and provide the employer confidence in your localized experience/training. Understanding the local labor market (which industries hire most, where the most jobs are predicted) can also help you to chart your course going forward in your career.

The best advice as you seek to enter and to advance in the U.S. workforce is to not lose hope for your professional goals. Refugees are the most resilient individuals I have ever encountered and are assets to any organization lucky enough to benefit from their determination and skills.

99

TRANSFERRED SPOUSES/PARTNERS

Companies often invest to relocate a leader to another country. The number one reason a relocation fails is that the family is unhappy. Finding ways for the transferred spouse/partner to get social and professional networks started is key to the family's success and the success of the employee's work career. Let's look at a few examples of how the future work skills of a transferred spouse/partner can be helped.

Case Studies:

MARISSA, PREVIOUSLY A LAWYER IN GERMANY

A large international company moves several people to the United States and our region every month. Many arrive with a spouse and children. The employee starts work immediately. The employee is already in the company network, excited, and motivated. In one case, the spouse, Marissa, had previously worked but most recently had been a homemaker in her home country. She arrived, got a new home set up, and got the children settled. Marissa was happy to make the move, but after six months was feeling lost. Her home was set up nicely, her kids were happy, and her husband's work was good. But what about her? She found out about the St. Louis Mosaic Project's women's network program and started to make friends. She joined an online book club with others. She considered how to connect her professional interests with a professional organization while she lived here, knowing that she was not going to have paid work but wanted to keep up with trends in her field for future work options.

MARIO, PREVIOUSLY AN ENGINEER IN MEXICO

Mario moved with his wife when she got a great job at a U.S. company. They were both engineers in their home country. She started work as soon as they got settled in their new home. Mario, however, had to wait for his work authorization. He was restless and feeling demoralized. He finally got his work authorization. With our help, he was able to shadow someone at a U.S. company in an engineering role for a few days to see the similarities and differences with his previous work. In fact, he was such a good observer that the company hired him as a contract worker and then, ultimately, as an employee. In addition, he joined a men's expat group, which meets occasionally for a beverage and some fun. He knows that this social group is good for his current state of mind, and it will help build his network if he needs to seek another job in the future.

ANISHA, PREVIOUSLY A SCIENTIST IN INDIA

Anisha moved with her husband. She had been a professional in her home country but knew it would take a long time to get work authorization in the U.S. As her husband got more and more excited about his new opportunities, she suffered mild depression and loneliness. She heard about a network we support of international women who meet to enjoy the region and each other. She joined and started to form new friendships. She joined a mentor program as well, in which she was matched for a one-year connection to a local woman who wanted to have more international exposure. Her new friends helped her get a volunteer job with an animal shelter, where she improved her English and made new friends. When she ultimately got her work authorization, her wide network helped her make work connections that resulted in a job offer. While the job was not as senior as the work she had left behind in her home country, it was a good way to have a first job in the U.S.

A company can spend several hundred thousand dollars on the move through visits, housing, training, and school expenses. But after the relocation services end a few months after the move, the family is often left on its own. The need for "aftercare" is key. Aftercare is the set of services that help the family after it moves to its new home. Organizations like the St. Louis Mosaic Project, Welcoming America members, and various International Institutes and other immigrant support organizations around the country offer many of these services and refer or provide families additional services in the community.

With the increased use of technologies like Zoom and webinars, spouses who will be moving to our region can be invited to join in some of activities before they even move here. This way they make a few friends and might have a local mentor or be in a local book club before arrival, so they feel positive about having a good experience after the family moves.

Volunteer experiences are great for a transplant. There are specific rules for visa compliance about the kinds of volunteering that are allowed and not allowed, so you may need to check in with an immigration lawyer. In general, the concept is that the volunteering must not be "work a U.S. citizen could be paid to do," such as office work. It must be altruistic, such as working with animals or assisting in your child's school, or hands-on service helping others.

Why is volunteering important for your happiness and future success? This benefits you for three reasons. You improve your English skills by interacting with other volunteers. You make new relationships that will benefit you with personal enjoyment or professional connections in the future. Lastly, you will have a meaningful role in your new home community that gives you a feeling of connection. If you don't have a connection to get your volunteer work started, just start doing the easiest volunteer experience that comes your way at your child's school or at a religious congregation. It is more important to just do something than to wait for a perfect fit for volunteer experience.

Another benefit of volunteer experience is that you can add it to your résumé if you start to look for paid work in the future. This shows a potential employer that you can work with others in the U.S. style and that you have good English skills. It demonstrates that you are reliable, motivated, and energetic. You can talk about the experience in professional terms, such as "Twice each week assisted at the Pacific High School library. Helped with organization of materials. Used customer service skills to assist users. Learned the technology to order supplies." This can help you attain a paying job. Remember that you are building your skills for your future benefit; this will cheer you even if you are not being paid.

Why This Works

There is a lot of stress involved in moving to another country. There is stress on the employee, the spouse, and the extended family. This is complicated when the accompanying partner also has the desire to work and keep up professional skills. The visa process makes this hard, and it can take a few years for a work authorization to occur. So keeping up your personal and professional connections, language skills, and attitude are all important. And attitude may be the hardest and most essential! Many transferred international people get discouraged in this process, which is understandable. Take the comments in this chapter to heart, because there is much still in your control. Understand that this advice helps you in the long run — even if the short run feels harsh and sad. Your life will truly work out better than it feels in the early months of your move. You are resilient and can do it!

Several years ago, Susan Gobbo formed a group for international women who had moved to our region. Her passion and dedication expanded this group to over 500 women who now love to be together! See what you can learn from Susan in this next segment and maybe start a group like this in your community. This group radiates fun and optimism!

EXPERT CONTRIBUTOR

Susan Gobbo, Community Leader & Co-Founder, St. Louis International Spouses Meetup Group

Moving from another country to the U.S. can be exciting and challenging for families, especially for the spouses of international professionals. It has been reported that the inability to adapt to the new cultural environment by one or several family members, mostly the accompanying spouses, largely contributes to expatriates' assignment failures in the business world.

The accompanying spouses have a different adaptation process compared to their partners. They often feel isolated if they are not studying or working. There are major causes that push many expat spouses well beyond their comfort zones: language and cultural barriers, lack of personal and professional satisfaction, financial dependence on their working partner, low self-esteem, identity loss, anxiety, depression, and no family or friends' support.

Most of these spouses are highly educated, with bachelor's, master's, or Ph.D. degrees, and have had successful careers in their country of origin. Over time, many can legally work in the U.S., so their adaptation and networks become very important.

The St. Louis International Spouses Meetup Group was co-founded by Susan Gobbo in 2016 based on her own experiences of being an expat spouse and her studies on this topic. This group provides support, friendship, and guidance to the international women who move to the St. Louis area. Members join in small groups for social and cultural gatherings, sightseeing, and other activities. The group invites professional speakers to talk about different topics from personal to professional skills improvement. It helps members find volunteer and networking opportunities that can open new doors for jobs. It includes the Professional Shadowing Program designed by Susan Gobbo to provide experience-based familiarity with the U.S. working environment for international spouses with work permits and assist them in closing their career gap.

Here are some informal tips suggested by the group that help accompanying spouses in their adaptation process:

- Learn the language and set short- and long-term goals.
- Develop new skills through courses and volunteering opportunities.
- Keep communication open with your partner so together you can feel comfortable discussing the difficulties you both may be facing.
- Look for support outside of the home; do not try to solve your problems alone.

- Have a routine and develop a schedule; participate in meaningful activities and exercise.

- Develop a network: find international social groups (you might find commonalities as outsiders that make you feel closer to home).

- Connect and integrate with the local community through neighbors, children's schools, organizations, programs, clubs, sports, religious groups, and local events.

- Be curious and open-minded to explore and learn about the culture and customs of the host culture.

- Keep a positive mentality and enjoy your new journey!

> 99

After the St. Louis International Spouses Meetup Group started, a well-connected community leader named Annie Schlafly met Susan Gobbo and they created a new group, called the International Mentoring Program — St. Louis, which brought local women together with international women. These two dedicated women match locals and internationals into pairs, and the results have been magical. The international woman gains a local friend and connections to networks for social or career benefits, while the local woman learns more about the world. There are over 150 matches to date, and the numbers keep growing. These friendships bond the newcomers to our region. Read Annie's description below; it might help you to find a local women's group that would love this kind of outreach.

EXPERT CONTRIBUTOR

Annie Schlafly, Community Leader & Co-Founder, International Mentoring Program — St. Louis

Moving to America as a foreign-born person can be an intimidating experience in many ways. The culture, language, food, social cues, and business etiquette may all be different from one's own country. Many internationals are finding jobs in American companies and choosing to move, but there are many obstacles to having a successful experience in their new city, apart from securing an excellent job in the states.

Over three years ago, The International Mentoring Program — St. Louis was created by Annie Schlafly and Susan Gobbo to address many of the issues faced by foreign-born community members moving to St. Louis. Each international woman arriving in St. Louis can become a member of the mentoring program. This year-long program is meant to accelerate her acclimation into the St. Louis community by being in a group of 10 women — five internationals and five locals — and paired with one of the locals in the group. These highly educated, extremely talented and skilled women are a real asset for any city.

Participation in the International Mentoring Program involves, among other things, the following:

1. Résumé building
2. Networking with St. Louis companies and their employees in their chosen field

3. Placement and service on non-profit boards throughout the St. Louis region

4. Ongoing work communication skills and adapting to the American culture

5. Social gatherings, such as a mayor's reception, attending sporting events, and holiday party

6. Creating lasting friendships and partnerships which ensure a successful transition and adaptation to their new city

The desired outcome for participants in the mentor program is that they and their families become a vital part of the St. Louis community by having friends and social connections, by obtaining a job (if desired and legally possible), and having such a positive experience that they choose to stay in St. Louis and give back to the city in a myriad of ways.

99

PROFESSIONAL CONNECTIONS AT THE EXECUTIVE LEVEL

You have moved ahead in the U.S. with your work experience and are now looking for a new job at a higher level. Your networking skill also needs to be at a higher level. You need to meet more people at the higher levels within companies. Let's look at ways to move your skills to a more advanced way of making professional connections.

Case Study:

ZEYNEP, A FINANCIAL DIRECTOR FROM TURKEY

Zeynep lost her director-level American job and was job hunting. Her specific expertise was narrow. She met with someone who heads a professional executive connector network in town. He had many ideas and possible connections to offer to her. He suggested that she broaden her financial description of her skills and desired jobs. She got a job offer in finance at one of the health centers in town but may follow up on some of the connections suggested by the professional connector to keep her future options open and build her professional network.

In this Midwest region, there are many business, cultural, and ethnic organizations. There are professional organizations for all fields. These offer a welcoming environment to attend seminars, hear speakers, and make positive working relationships through shared interests. How can you find these organizations? Search online by your city and your profession or industry. Use LinkedIn to search their directory of groups. When you learn of someone who has a skill set like yours, reach out with a question, such as "I see you are a marketing professional. As a relative newcomer with a marketing and advertising background new to this city, what two organizations should I join?"

Some organizations will be free; others may have a membership fee. If you are not working outside the home, you may feel that you cannot spend the money to pay the annual dues. Those are personal choices, but consider this: If you seek a director or executive-level position, you should spend the money for one professional organization for a year and consider it an investment in your career over the long term. Then make it worth the investment by getting involved. Once you join, attend meetings and be part of a committee. Committees are where you will get to know others by working together. The experience will be valuable to improve your language skills specific to your field and will allow you to make professional connections in a comfortable way. Lastly, it will keep you up to date on what is new in your field.

Why This Works

The professional world is changing quickly. Whether you are skilled in art material restoration, physical therapy, or accounting, the language and tools keep evolving for your field. You want to keep up with this. It makes you feel like your best professional self, as your work is part of your personal identity that you do not want to leave behind. And if you are not yet authorized to work but expect to be in the future, it enables you to leverage those connections to network towards a job in your field. As a working person, you obviously invested a lot of time and money earlier to achieve your previous work experience and earnings. In this stage of your American career, you need to build on that in different ways to protect your earning power for your future and for the future financial health of your family.

A respected executive connector, Ram Lakshmanan, shares his knowledge from being a leader of an organization called Executive Connections St. Louis. He believes this program is key to his having maximum impact on highly skilled people in our region who need the tools and motivation to get their next executive-level job.

EXPERT CONTRIBUTOR

Ram Lakshmanan, President, Executive Connections St. Louis

There are many organizations in the U.S. that offer opportunities to network with professionals, business owners, and investors. For example, there are ExecuNet, chambers of commerce, ACG (Association for Corporate Growth), BNI (Business Network International), SCORE, AMA (American Marketing Association), Rotary International, Young Entrepreneur Council, and so on. They provide powerful opportunities to connect with key decision makers and other highly connected professionals. Investing time and effort in building these connections will in turn yield further people connections as well as potential job leads — sometimes even before they are advertised. That provides the hunter a significant advantage!

A good example of powerful networking is Executive Connections (EC) St. Louis. This professional network accepts members based on certain criteria. Their URL is: **https://www.executiveconnectionsstl.org/member-criteria.html** Admitted members get instant access to industry-leading executives in St. Louis who are "alumni" of EC. They are generous givers and powerful connectors. They generously help their fellow EC members with advice, guidance, powerful networking connections, recommendations, and mentoring support on an ongoing basis. The core values of Executive Connections are networking for life and giving more than you receive. The following lists are their top recommendations:

1. Networking is a life skill of developing relationships with people over extended periods of time.

    » It is not shaking hands, trading business cards and emails, or having coffee together.

    » There is give and take involving efforts on both parties.

    » It's getting to a point of not only whom you know and who knows you, but how well you know each other.

2. Networking is not a plea for help.

    » Get over this mental barrier.

    » Networking is exchanging ideas, sharing resources, meeting and learning about new people, and building relationships.

    » Over a period of time, both sides gain from the experience of knowing each other and possibly from helping each other.

3. The six-touch rule: For a relationship to start building, you need at least six touches:

- » First touch: A phone call to set up a meeting
- » Second touch: An invitation to connect on LinkedIn (with some people, this could happen after the fourth touch mentioned below)
- » Third touch: Meeting face to face
- » Fourth touch: A follow-up email that summarizes the meeting, referrals, and other items discussed
- » Fifth touch: The thank-you note/card you send after the meeting
- » Sixth touch: A follow-up phone call after meeting with the referrals

The more effective and reinforcing each touch is, the stronger the relationship.

4. Nurture the relationship:

- » Treat each referral like gold. It is precious. Handle it carefully. When I provide a referral, I am giving you a piece of me/my personal reputation. If you do a good job, my reputation is enhanced. If you don't, my reputation may take a hit. Do your best to enhance the reputation — yours as well as mine.
- » Share periodic updates on your search. Do this via emails (in most cases), phone calls, or face-to-face meetings. Which communication method should you use? The simple rule is: The stronger the relationship or the more assistance a person provided, the more personal the contact should be. A phone call or a personal meeting will bring out grateful emotions and non-verbal cues.

- » Definitely share your news when you are hired and thank the contacts. Here is a great opportunity to thank each hiring manager and other great contacts for their interest and help and update them on your success; and let them know that you would like to stay in touch in the future. Thus, they will become a part of your network.
- » You may choose to classify your network of contacts into an:
  Acquaintance — know only slightly
  Associate — professional and/or social relationship
  Ally — mutually supportive relationship
  Advocate — would intercede on your behalf (and you may do likewise)

Periodically drop a note to your networking contacts or call some of them to inquire about their welfare. Make use of occasions like Easter, July 4th, Christmas, etc., or their birthdays or anniversaries if you happen to know them closely. Take the opportunity to send a message if you see them post a LinkedIn update on a new position/promotion, or to provide an article or book recommendation.

Remember your network is like a muscle. The more you work it, the stronger it gets. Both frequency and quality of interactions are important.

5. Extra credits:
- » Go out of your way to appreciate your network contacts. Send them a small gift or a thank-you note just as a surprise.

- » Provide business or career networking leads to your contacts confidentially and let them decide how they want to handle the leads.

- » Help your contacts in times of need when you hear of them. E.g., possible job loss, death in their family, or some other emergency. Go beyond the professional connections to personal connections — of course, with due respect to their privacy and personal space.

From being a "Networker," strive to become a "Connector." You become more valuable to others.

LINKEDIN EXPERTISE IN DEPTH

Earlier in the book, there were examples of the importance of using LinkedIn, and some basic tips to get started. Because you have already advanced in your role and your job search skills, here is more detailed advice about how to use this important job search and job advancement tool to keep you "always ready" in the event of an unexpected opportunity or connection.

Case Study:

FAIZAN, A CONSULTANT FROM PAKISTAN

Faizan lost his highly paid job in the U.S. and was working hard to get his next position. He studied key jobs to get his LinkedIn profile right. He listed job accomplishments to show that he wanted to connect to the right kinds of people and opportunities. He started to personalize his LinkedIn requests and got better industry contacts to help in his job search. He reached out via a personalized invitation to connect based on his interests, and about half those he invited responded in a positive way (he did not hear from the others at all, but that was okay). He "followed" more people in his field regionally and began commenting on their postings. He saw LinkedIn webinars and group meetings in his field that he signed up to attend. He ultimately got a new job that came from this process.

Using LinkedIn takes a lot of time and attention. Like any skill, you will get better at it as you work on it every day for your professional benefit. Keep up with new functionality at LinkedIn, such as new ways to indicate that you are open to work or that you have a specific skill certification. They keep adding new trainings and ways to leverage their networks among people, companies, and industries.

Kathy Bernard teaches LinkedIn skills for companies and other organizations that want their people to take their professional images and connections to an executive level. See if her recommendations make you want to revise your

LinkedIn profile and create a more dynamic experience for yourself using LinkedIn.

❝

EXPERT CONTRIBUTOR

Kathy Bernard, CEO, LinkedIn Trainer and Career Coach, WiserU

LinkedIn can be a huge help in your job search because through it, you can network with supportive people, apply for jobs, and impress recruiters looking for qualified candidates. Here's how to maximize your LinkedIn presence.

1. **Create a strong LinkedIn profile** to show that you are a viable candidate for the jobs that you want.

    » Include the job titles that you want in your headline and in your About summary. Add your phone number or email address into your summary to make it easy to contact you.

    » If unemployed, add a current entry into your Experience section, since some companies only consider employed people. Include job titles that you want in the Job Title box. Make the company name "Available." In the Location box, add your current or target city. In the Date boxes, make the "From month" the month after you left your last job, then click the "I currently work here" box. Uncheck "Update my headline" to keep LinkedIn from shortening your headline. Use the 2,000-character description box to list all the duties that you can do based on job descriptions for jobs that you want. Instead of stating that you're currently doing such duties, use phrase like "Able to manage...," "Adept at handling...," "or "Highly skilled at..." to show that you can do such work.

> » Maximize your past job experience entries to closely match the jobs that you want.

> » Indicate languages that you speak and write in the Language section, but list English first so employers will trust that you're fluent. If you aren't fluent, take courses to improve.

> » If people in the U.S. find your name difficult to pronounce, consider adding a nickname to your profile name box and on your résumé. Example: Dahye (Debbie) Kim. Or use the "Add Name Pronunciation" feature on the LinkedIn mobile app to gives recruiters confidence to call you by name.

2. **Have at least 100 LinkedIn connections** in the U.S. to ensure employers that you're already in-country. Mention in your invitations if you have mutual connections. For example, write "I see that we have [NUMBER] of mutual connections. You must be someone I should know!"

3. **Invite people from your country** who are now living and working in the United States to connect. Ask them how they landed the job with their company. If you'd be a good fit for their organization, ask them to refer you for open positions. Sometimes companies will pay them for their referrals, so they'll benefit too.

4. **Be active on LinkedIn.**

    » Join LinkedIn groups in your industry, field, and target cities so that recruiters can find you. Join LinkedIn groups for open networkers or "LIONs" (LinkedIn open networkers) and invite Americans from these groups to connect. Open networkers accept almost all invitations.

    » Follow hundreds of target companies to alert them of your interest.

    » Apply for jobs through the LinkedIn Jobs tab.

5. **Customize your LinkedIn invitations** to explain why you want to connect, but don't mention wanting a job at their company in your invitation.

    » Don't use words like "Dear Mrs. (NAME)" or "Madam/Sir" or flowery words like "Dearest." Instead, use the person's first name and get to your point. Example: "Bob, we're both in the same LinkedIn group for financial analysts. I've enjoyed your group discussions. Let's connect!"

    » Once you've established the connection, send a follow-up message. Example: "Bob, thanks for accepting my invitation. I'm seeking a sales position here in Dallas, so if you hear of opportunities, please let me know."

6. **State your employment status** for working in the U.S. — companies need to know before hiring!

7. Apply for jobs at **companies where they have offices or headquarters in your home** country or where speaking your native language is a plus. Also, mention on your profile if

you have already worked internationally and where. This will help convince people that you can work internationally.

8. **Reach out to organizations** like the St. Louis Mosaic Project that help foreign-born people land jobs in your city.

9. **Focus on big companies with the money** and infrastructure to hire you. Typically, large companies in large cities on the East and West Coasts are your best options. Some industries, like healthcare and tech, are often more able to hire foreign-born applicants in any city.

10. **Start applying early,** don't expect miracles, and don't give up. Even though you may have to work 10 times harder to get a job than people born in the U.S., those who succeed try the hardest.

99

CREDENTIALS

How to Evaluate and Translate the Value of Your Degrees

There are organizations that will evaluate your prior credentials and issue an evaluation showing how your prior work compares to American degrees. This will truly boost your confidence in your application process.

Case Study:

HARU, A MECHANICAL ENGINEER FROM KOREA

Haru had an advanced degree, but companies she spoke with did not know how it compared to a similar degree from a U.S. institution. This lessened Haru's confidence. It worried her that she would have to take coursework all over again. She worked with one of several organizations who evaluate credentials to have her credentials reviewed and a comparison document prepared. She was able to attach this to her job applications. She brought this to her interviews. With these documents in hand, the HR professionals were able to reassure the hiring managers that she would perform the work well. Having this credential evaluation performed and available was a real relief for Haru. She was able to be more focused on the job search knowing she had a way to show her true expertise and would not need to repeat her earlier degree work for the U.S. market.

Looking at the case study above, Haru might have used WES, World Education Services, to have her credentials reviewed. See how Paul Feltman describes how this might be of value to you.

EXPERT CONTRIBUTOR

Paul Feltman, Deputy Executive Director, Global Talent Bridge, World Education Services

If you earned a university degree or diploma before coming to the United States, you may be wondering if your education will be useful in helping you find a job here. Are international degrees recognized by U.S. employers? Do you need a degree from an American university to qualify for a job in the U.S.? Understanding a process called credential evaluation can guide your next steps.

A credential evaluation can help ensure that the degrees, diplomas, and certificates you earned outside of the U.S. are understood by employers in this country. The evaluation process creates a report with information about your international credentials and their U.S. equivalency. This report can demonstrate to prospective employers that you meet the requirements for a position. However, because the credential evaluation process is not familiar to many U.S. employers—and prospective employers ultimately decide whether they accept an evaluation report—it is important that job seekers understand how to secure a valid credential evaluation and use it during their job search.

How does the process work?

Here are tips on how to select a credential evaluation service, navigate the steps of the process, and share the results of your report with prospective employers.

1. Research employer requirements for evaluation. Not all U.S. employers are familiar with the credential evaluation process, but some companies that frequently hire internationally educated candidates, including immigrants and refugees, may have established requirements for evaluation. Check the company's website or job posting for information. If you are in touch with a recruiter, ask about their requirements. If you cannot find information about credential evaluation, it is likely that the company does not have a preferred process. The steps below will help you request and use a credential evaluation.

2. Select the right credential evaluation agency. In some countries, credential evaluation is done by a government agency. In the U.S., the process is done by private, non-profit organizations and companies. There are many credential evaluation services available in the U.S., but not all are reliable or widely accepted. The National Association of Credential Evaluation Services (NACES) provides a list of reputable services on its website, **www.NACES.org.** When selecting a credential evaluation service, it is important to understand costs, timeframe, and process for the evaluation. The most credible credential evaluation services require that applicants submit official copies of academic credentials for evaluation. This "authentication" may add time to the evaluation process but is more widely recognized by U.S. employers.

3. Determine the type of evaluation you need. Credential evaluation services provide various types of reports for different purposes. A "basic" report, sometimes called a document-by-document report, provides the U.S. equivalency of academic credentials attained abroad. A "detailed," or course-by-course report, includes the U.S. equivalency of your courses, grades, and calculation of grade point average (GPA). A basic report is often sufficient for employment

purposes, as it demonstrates to the employer that the candidate meets the educational requirements for a job. When selecting the type of evaluation you need, check the "lifetime" of the report. Some reports are only valid for a certain timeframe. Others do not expire, meaning you can use them for future job applications or other purposes.

4. Obtain required documents. The evaluation service you select will provide detailed instructions on required documents and how to submit them. The most reputable credential evaluation services will require official versions of academic credentials that you earned outside of the U.S. for evaluation. These official documents must be issued by recognized educational institutions, translated into English, and signed and sealed by authorized officials. To avoid delays in completing your credential evaluation, it is important to carefully follow instructions and to request official documents from your academic institution as early as possible. Some evaluation services can receive documents electronically, which significantly speeds up the process.

5. Receive your completed report. The credential evaluation service will verify the authenticity of your documents, measure your credentials against U.S. standards, and create a report. The report can be delivered directly to identified recipients. However, for your job search, you should request a copy of the report for yourself to share with prospective employers.

6. Use your report in your job search. The U.S. equivalency of your academic credentials can be helpful in starting the first stages of your job search. Locate the equivalency statement on your evaluation report; it is a sentence like "Evaluated by [name of credential evaluation service], as equivalent to a four-year U.S. bachelor's degree." Include this statement in your cover letter and on your résumé. You can also bring

your credential evaluation report to job interviews to provide the employer with proof of your academic accomplishments. Some credential evaluation services offer digital tools to display your credentials on social media, including professional networking platforms like LinkedIn.

What else can you do with a credential evaluation? Once your evaluation is complete, you can use it to meet other career goals in the U.S., including applying for professional licensure or further education. Confirm the "lifetime" of your report to ensure it does not expire.

- **APPLY FOR A LICENSE:** In the U.S., many professional fields, including healthcare, architecture, engineering, and education, require licenses for certain careers. These licenses are awarded by professional licensing boards within each state that establish their own requirements for credential evaluations, examinations, and work experience. Before applying for a license, consult your local licensing board to understand what type of credential evaluation is required. Some licensing boards conduct evaluations themselves; others may require that you use a specific external service.

- **APPLY FOR FURTHER EDUCATION:** A credential evaluation is often a required part of a college or university admissions application. Admissions officers will refer to the evaluation to determine if you meet requirements for admissions or to transfer earned credits. With a credential evaluation, you can save time and money by not having to repeat courses that you have already completed outside of the U.S. However, some academic institutions have limitations on how many international credits they accept. You can contact the admissions office to learn their policy.

How much does a credential evaluation cost? The cost of an evaluation depends upon many factors, including the report type and processing time. Fees for "basic" reports typically range from USD $90 to $160; "detailed" reports range from $150 to $420. Your university may charge fees to issue official copies of your transcripts or provide translations for evaluation. There may also be a cost to request additional copies of the report or to pay for expedited processing.

Some credential evaluation services provide free tools to help you start the process. World Education Services offers tools to preview your degree equivalency or GPA online before requesting official reports. You can access these tools at **www.wes.org/wes-tools/**.

Upwardly Global is a national organization that stands out for its work advising and placing foreign-born job seekers who have a college degree from outside the U.S. Let's learn more and see if they and their online materials might help you.

UPWARDLY GLOBAL

If you have been in the U.S. for seven years or fewer and have a college degree from outside the U.S., Upwardly Global may be able to connect you to jobs across the U.S. Another organization, Welcome Back, works in several regions around the

U.S. to get former medically trained professionals back into the medical field.

Case Study:

GUILLAUME, A MARKETING MANAGER FROM FRANCE

Guillaume was having a hard time locating a new job in his city in the U.S. He was willing to move for the right job. Despite having good work experience and knowledge, he did not have a support network to help him in his search. He read about data showing that many companies wanted the kind of expertise he had, but he did not know which specific companies might appreciate his global outlook. He heard about Upwardly Global, an organization that connects work-authorized internationals with companies looking for talent. He fit their criteria for assistance and was relieved to have a person assigned to connect him directly to employers who wanted his level of work experience and international marketing skills. Upwardly Global helped rewrite his résumé, prepped him for interviews, and arranged interviews that led to a job. Guillaume moved across the country to fulfill his American work dream.

EXPERT CONTRIBUTOR
The Upwardly Global Team

Over 20+ years, Upwardly Global has witnessed the tremendous talent and experience that immigrants and refugees bring to the United States. You bring educational degrees, meaningful professional backgrounds, skills that match the needs of industries experiencing significant growth, innovative perspectives, multiple languages, and deep cultural competency in an increasingly global world. Despite that, more than two million immigrant, refugee, and asylee professionals like yourself end up facing systemic barriers while navigating the job search, resulting in unemployment or "survival jobs" that are low paid and do not lead to advancement. For more information on this, see: **"Leaving Money on the Table: The Persistence of Brain Waste among College-Educated Immigrants"** [https://www.migrationpolicy.org/sites/default/files/publications/mpi-brain-waste-analysis-june2021-final.pdf]

Upwardly Global was the first national organization founded to precisely address this disparity — and we have dedicated ourselves to understanding and helping those we work with to eliminate employment barriers so your skills and perspectives are included in the American workforce.

Upwardly Global has connected with and helped thousands of talented immigrants and refugees rebuild their lives and professional careers in the U.S. and helped them to earn starting salaries of $60,000 on average.

Here are a few of the key tips that can help you in your job search:

Know who's hiring and stay informed about your industry: Hunt for companies that are hiring on platforms such as Indeed and Glassdoor and pay attention to the words they use to describe positions. Read about your industry, join online conversations, and follow industry leaders to see how demand is shifting. There are more sophisticated tools as well, like Emsi and Burning Glass Technologies, that show labor market trends, sought after credentials, and more in real time — organizations like Upwardly Global can help you access that information.

Continue developing your skills: Take new courses or apply for new certifications in your industry through online platforms like Coursera and keep updating your résumé to show that your knowledge is not static in a fast-paced environment. There are also complicated procedures for relicensing that are required in a number of fields. Upwardly Global has a list of licensing guides (**www.upwardlyglobal.org/programs/professional-licensing-guides**) that are updated every few years on our website that can be a helpful guide through these complex processes. In some cases, we also recommend considering alternative career pathways that allow you to utilize many of your skills in an adjacent field.

Increase confidence with interviewing: Many job applications include an interview component. Research common interview practices and prepare using mock interview sessions. We've made our most popular courses, created especially for immigrants, available for free online at this URL: **www.upwardlyglobal.org/free-online-job-search-courses.**

Build your network: It may seem extraneous, but it is not. Some 85% of people in the United States get their jobs through a connection. Attend job fairs, be active (and always professional) on social media, attend networking events, and arrange informational interviews. Your online presence is especially important so strengthen your profiles (**https://jobversity.upwardlyglobal.org/wp-content/uploads/2020/11/Best-things-you-can-do-to-make-your-LinkedIn-profile-stand-out-to-recruiters.pdf**) and start connecting.

Join a career skills program: Engaging with a free career skills program like Upwardly Global provides you with support across all of these verticals:

- individualized, job-centered coaching by people familiar with immigrants and with the U.S. market

- opportunities to take classes and earn credentials — many for free — and to understand licensing needed in highly specialized fields

- connections to mentors who have expertise and connections in your industry and to placement opportunities

The U.S. non-profit field is a robust part of how our economy and social service sector work — and you should not hesitate to turn to it for support and connection. We understand that the job-searching process can at times feel long and frustrating. Continue to reach out to employers, seek resources for support, and remain hopeful in the process. If you are interested, check out Upwardly Global's application page at **www.upwardlyglobal.org/programs/application-apply-now.**

We are so happy that you have come to the United States — we embrace you with open arms, and we know our country is lucky to have your skills, talent, experience, and innovation. We welcome you to be in touch and wish you good luck!

SUMMARY OF STAGE VI
Special Knowledge

These final sections brought forward unique expertise to help your progress in the workplace. It is important to keep your contacts and relationships active, as well as keep your LinkedIn profile updated. You will likely continue to use a variety of resources as you grow in your job and career.

CONCLUSION

You are destined to succeed. If you use the ideas suggested in this guide along with the advice of experts who know your community more deeply, you will get your American job and advance in your career. Remember that there are people and organizations who welcome you and want you to succeed. Let them help you, and then you can help others in the future.

Finding a job and growing in your career are each very personal. Your path is unique. Your interactions are unique. What works for you is unique. Pick out the points most relevant to your situation from the case studies in this book. Use the resources listed in the back to learn more or to make a direct connection.

The United States welcomes you, and those of us devoted to this work welcome you as well. By following advice provided here, you will be on the path to get hired and to advance in your American career.

GOOD LUCK!

USE THIS SPACE TO TAKE NOTES

Acknowledgments

I would like to thank...

The St. Louis Economic Development Partnership team at the World Trade Center St. Louis, who have helped build the knowledge that helps international people in St. Louis to thrive: Rodney Crim, Tim Nowak, Stella Sheehan-Coen, Sean Mullins, Suzanne Sierra, Bomi Park, Susan Spitz, and Karen Gentles.

The original supporters of the research that led to the founding of the St. Louis Mosaic Project: David Kemper, Dee Joyner, Molly Hyland, Bob Fox, Maxine Clark, Denny Coleman, Joe Reagan, and Anna Crosslin.

Community members who go above and beyond with connections and support for foreign-born people: Sorin Vaduva, Susan Gobbo, Annie Schlafly, Kent Hirschfelder, Peter Tao, Caroline Fan, Rick Shang, Stuart Bradley, Anthony Bartlett, Ness Sandoval, Daniela Velasquez, Fran Levine, Naretha Hopson, Paul Tice, John Beuerlein, Bryan Lawrence, Sekhar Prabhakar, Vin Ko and others.

Business supporters, chambers of commerce, university, and cultural groups in St. Louis, including Karlos Ramirez, Alejandro Santiago, Alex Lee, Al Li, Thong Tarm, Geoffrey Soyiantet, Segun Babalosa, Akif Cogo, Jason Hall, Sarah Arnosky, Valerie Patton, Steve Johnson, Jim Alexander,

Mark Wrighton, Hank Webber, Julia Macias, Ed Macias, Diego Abente, and Jorge Riopedre.

The St. Louis Regional Business Council and Kathy Osborn for the commitment to international students and their connections with mentors.

The immigration attorneys with whom I work: Legal Services of Eastern Missouri, David Glaser, Jessica Mayo, Nicole Cortes, Martha Hereford, Jim Hacking, Diane Metzger, Nalini Mahadaven, Pari Sheth, Melanie Tuey, Kenneth Schmitt, Javad Khazaeli, and Patavee Vanadilok.

The Welcoming America team that creates and builds welcoming programs for immigrant inclusion across the country, including Rachel Perić, David Lubell, Meg Shoemaker, Christina Pope, Molly Hilligoss, Lola Pak, and Leyla Compani.

The Welcoming Economies colleagues who welcome international people to the heartland of the country: Steve Tobocman, Guiqiu Wang, Gracie Xavier, Sloan Herrick, Sanjita Pradhan, Gurinder Hohl, Guadalupe Velasquez, Sabeen Nasim, Peter Gonzales, Brittany Ford, Bryan Warren, Sloan Herrick, Eva Hassett, Karen Phillippi, Susan Downs-Karkos, and Nicole Pumphrey.

The International Institute of St. Louis team that serves over 6,000 foreign-born people annually with a range of services and provides the majority of our region's refugee resettlement support: Arrey Obenson, Blake Hamilton, Paul Costigan, Chelsea Hand-Sheridan, Anita Barker, Kelly Moore, Carrie Brickey, Ariel Burgess, and Aziza Mirkhanova.

ACKNOWLEDGMENTS

The St. Louis Immigrant Service Providers Network, including Meredith Rataj, Rita Chang, and the dozens of agencies that serve our foreign-born community.

Special friends who have shared their international stories and lives with me: Ola Ayeni, Yemi Akande-Bartsch, Ravi Kyasaram, Tarini Varma, Sumit Verma, Sekhar Prabhakar, Xiayao Li, Peichuan Sun, Javier Detrinidad and Zellipah Githua plus many more.

Thanks to my early readers and supporters, including Susanne Evens, Nalini Mahadevan, Susan Gobbo, Todd Schulte, Claudia Romo Edelman, Bob Kolf, Kurt Dirks, Lauren Herring, Craig Montuori, Amanda Bergson-Shilcock, Stephen Yale-Loehr, Jeremy Robbins, Alex Lee, and Gabriela Ramírez-Arellano.

My insightful and knowledgeable book advisor, Bonnie Daneker and team, including Becky Bayne and Andrew Doty.

And most importantly, my family, including my supportive husband, Dr. Bruce Cohen, and children Greg and Lauren Cohen, Scott and Emma Cohen, and my mom, Sue Marcus.

About the Author

Betsy Cohen is the Executive Director of the St. Louis Mosaic Project, a program of the World Trade Center St. Louis within the St. Louis Economic Development Partnership. The goal is to attract and retain international people to St. Louis for their skills and cultures to add to our population and diversity. This work is done through collaborations with hundreds of local organizations, universities, corporations, cultural groups, faith organizations, K–12 schools, immigration agencies, and government entities. Betsy has mentored and advised international students, international executives, and hundreds of foreign-born people, work-authorized job seekers personally and through social media. Betsy has worked with hundreds of international people in their job searches and career advancement.

Betsy had an extensive corporate career in marketing at an international consumer goods company. She is a graduate of Wellesley College and the Harvard Business School. She is on the advisory board for the St. Louis University Chaifetz School of Business and on the Cortex Innovation Community committee for diversity, equity, and inclusion. Previously, she served on other community boards and committees and ran a regional network. She was recognized as a Most Influential Businesswoman by the *St. Louis Business Journal* and as a Woman Business Leader by the YWCA.

In 2021, she was recognized by the National Conference for Community and Justice of Metro St. Louis for promoting respect among diverse communities.

Betsy is available for consultations, group presentations, or webinars.

Please see new content at:

www.linkedin.com/company/welcomeyouarehired/about

www.welcomeyouarehired.com

www.linkedin.com/in/betsyhcohen

Resources

Stage I: Understanding the Job Search

Book: *Take Control of your Job Search: 10 Emotions You Must Master to Land the Job* by Lauren Herring, 2020.

Stage II: Pre-Job Interview Tools and Tips

Resume Examples and Sample Resumes for 2021 (www.indeed.com)

CV vs. Resume: What's the Difference? (www.MSN.com)

How Employers Use Applicant Tracking Systems (ATS) (www.thebalancecareers.com)

How to write the best resume for artificial intelligence and robots (www.CNBC.com)

Use this one-paragraph cover letter to land your next job interview (www.fastcompany.com)

Cover Letter Samples and Templates (www.indeed.com)

Immigrants Who 'Americanized' Their Names Earned 14 Percent More, Study Says (www.parade.com)

Immigrant Career Pathways — International Institute of St. Louis (www.iistl.org)

International Professionals Program — The Welcoming Center

How to Increase Your Odds of Success with a Warm Introduction (www.forbes.com)

What Is LinkedIn and Why Should You Be on It? (www.lifewire.com)

WiserU — Kathy Bernard, LinkedIn and Career Trainer

Maximizing LinkedIn for Foreign-Born Job Seekers and International Students by Kathy Kaegel Bernard

E-Book: Ever-Appropriate Etiquette: 5 Steps to the Professional Presence that Pays by Naretha Hopson, 2015.

Vistaprint online printing services: business cards, signage and more

Custom online business printing and design | MOO U.S.

Job Search | Indeed

Glassdoor Job Search | Find the job that fits your life

Salary.com salary calculator, salary comparison, and compensation data

....

Stage III: Interview Process and Preparation

myvisajobs.com — solution for work visa, student visa, visa jobs, and green cards

Panel Interview Questions, Answers, and Tips (www.thebalancecareers.com)

STAR Interview Method: The Ultimate Guide (https://blog.hubspot.com)

50 Most Common Interview Questions | Glassdoor

How to brag in an interview without sounding conceited (www.fastcompany.com)

How to Ask Someone to be a Reference | Examples (www.resume.com)

4 Sample Thank-You Emails for After an Interview (www.indeed.com)

How to write the best thank-you note after a job interview (www.fastcompany.com)

....

Stage IV: Job Acceptance

Negotiating a Job Offer? Here's How to Get What You Want. (https://hbr.org)

Job Shadowing: What Is It? (www.thebalancecareers.com)

Adult Internships — A Way to Experience a New Career (www.thebalancecareers.com)

AILA's Immigration Lawyer Search (www.ailalawyer.com)

....

Stage V: Advancing Your Workplace Career

Mentor vs. Sponsor | Leader's Edge Magazine (www.leadersedge.com)

Why Likability Matters More at Work — *WSJ*

Employee Resource Groups | Diversity and Inclusion | PeopleScout

Toot Your Own Horn At Work | (www.monster.com)

What Does DEI Mean in the Workplace? | Built In

DAP | Diversity Awareness Partnership St. Louis (https://dapinclusive.org)

Stage VI: Special Knowledge—International Students

Global Talent Retention Initiative Global Detroit (https://globaldetroitmi.org)

St. Louis Mosaic Project | International Student Resources for Hiring (www.stlmosaicproject.org)

Book: *Power Ties: The International Student's Guide to Finding a Job in the United States* by Dan Beaudry, 2014.

Refugees

Refugee Career Pathways | The Administration for Children and Families (www.acf.hhs.gov)

Career Path — International Institute of St. Louis (www.iistl.org)

UNHCR — US Resettlement Partners

International Institute of St. Louis — Immigrant Services & Community Engagement Hub since 1919 (www.iistl.org)

Transferred Spouses/Partners

Avert Assignment Failure: Support Spouses in Overseas Relocations | (https://blog.SHRM.org)

The real cost of expatriate assignment failure | FIDI

Why 40% of Overseas Assignments Fail and What You Can Do to Prevent It (https://insights.learnlight.com)

St. Louis International Spouses Meetup (Saint Louis, MO) | Meetup

International Mentoring Program — St. Louis (https://sites.google.com/view/stlismentor)

Aftercare, a core function in Investment Promotion

Professional Connections

Executive Connections St. Louis (www.executiveconnectionsstl.org)

St. Louis Mosaic Project | Mosaic Project Professional Connectors (www.stlmosaicproject.org)

Professional Connection » Global Cleveland

....

LinkedIn Expertise in Depth

WiserU — Kathy Bernard, LinkedIn and Career Trainer and link to her e-book on this topic

Credentialing

Home — World Education Services (www.wes.org)

NACES | National Association of Credential Evaluation Services

....

Upwardly Global and Other Pathways

Immigrant & Refugee Professionals Career Services | Upwardly Global

Welcome Back Initiative for healthcare professionals

Book: *4 Weeks to Your American Dream Job* by Michael Patrick Miller, 2013.

Book: *My American Job* by Jacob J. Sapochnick, Esq., 2015.

COVER LETTER EXAMPLE
(not related to résumé example)

Dear Hiring Professional,

I would like to express my interest in the "Executive Assistant to the President" role. I am an exceptional fit for this position with my degree in Communication, my extensive top-level, strategic, executive-level assistant experience, combined with my ability to create relationships both across and outside of the institutions I worked for. I have a vision for making the President's life easier: Thinking ahead of what's next even before he/she does, being a liaison for the office, and having someone reliable right there.

I prepared company presentations, annual and quarterly reports, performed contract management, managed meetings, organized business and social events, and assisted the Business Development Manager in assessment of new business.

One of my key strengths is my ability to forge strong connections, as evidenced by being hired by my current employer in the U.S. My interest in working for your cultural organization is driven by my personal interaction and the recognition of the great contributions to the community by the institution. When I moved to town, your organization was one of the first places I visited. It was a wonderful way of getting acclimated with the city. I learned so much about the region. Your exhibit YY was my most memorable visit. I personally believe that your organization plays a major role in bringing the diverse communities of this metropolitan area together.

I am committed to serving the community alongside your organization in its inspiring mission, leadership in education, exploration, and contributing to its core value of inclusivity in the role of Executive Assistant to the President.

Yours,
ZZZZZ

RÉSUMÉ EXAMPLE

Example provided by Anita Barker, International Institute of St. Louis

---

ANIKA GIRMAY

St. Louis, MO
(314) 123-4567 | anika.girmay123@gmail.com
Permanent Resident – no visa sponsorship necessary

PROFESSIONAL SUMMARY

Detail-oriented Civil Engineer with 4 years of experience working in the public sector. Skilled in construction management and design. Effective project manager; experienced in providing cost estimates and finishing projects under budget and ahead of schedule. Resilience, flexibility, and ability to work successfully in an American work environment shown in work experience since relocation to the U.S.

CIVIL ENGINEERING EXPERIENCE

Foreign City Construction Office   *Foreign City, Ethiopia*
Supervisor   *2012 – 2015*

- Conducted supervision of construction projects on government sites including clinics and schools; achieved savings of more than $300,000 in clinic construction costs
- Used AutoCAD design software to produce structural drawings of buildings in line with government standards
- Ensured contractor use of quality materials and in accordance with design
- Ensured contractor work followed safety and environmental regulations
- Prepared cost estimates for materials, equipment, and labor

Foreign City University   *Foreign City, Ethiopia*
Assistant Lecturer   *2010 – 2012*

- Taught two general engineering courses to 1st year undergraduate Engineering (Engineering Mechanics and Engineering Skills)
- Prepared and taught lessons using PPT slides
- Graded papers and tests
- Attended meetings with students and other lecturers

Foreign City Public Works Construction Office   *Foreign City, Ethiopia*
Student Intern   *Oct 2009 – Jan 2010*

EDUCATION

Bachelor of Science in Civil Engineering *Foreign City, Ethiopia*
Foreign City University *July 2011*

ADDITIONAL WORK EXPERIENCE

Cookie Company, Inc. *St. Louis, MO*
QA Technician *February 2017–Present*

- Test and inspect cookies at different stages of production
- Check quality of cookies to ensure food quality standards are met
- Examine and inspect packaging to ensure code dates and packaging specifications are met
- Record test results and check reports for accuracy
- Ensure proper removal of damaged cookies or packages
- Ensure cleanliness of containers, materials, supplies, and work areas

Feeder *2015–2017*
- Weigh and count cookies
- Feed cookies into the packaging machines
- Move controls to start, stop and adjust production equipment
- Remove and properly dispose of damaged cookies or packages
- Clean containers, materials, supplies, or work areas, using cleaning solutions and hand tools

SKILLS & ABILITIES

Effective management and teamwork skills
Strong communication and critical thinking skills
AutoCAD, Windows XP/7/8/10, Microsoft Office tools
(including Word, Excel, PowerPoint, Outlook)

Languages: English, Amharic (native)

CPSIA information can be obtained
at www.ICGtesting.com
Printed in the USA
FSHW021838041121
85920FS